CSCB 498-41

SO-DTB-788

Microcomputer Interfacing With the 8255 PPI Chip

by
Paul F. Goldsbrough
With
Portions of the Experiments by
Peter R. Rony

Howard W. Sams & Co., Inc.
4300 WEST 62ND ST. INDIANAPOLIS, INDIANA 46268 USA

Copyright © 1979 by Paul F. Goldsbrough

FIRST EDITION
FIRST PRINTING—1979

All rights reserved. No part of this book shall be
reproduced, stored in a retrieval system, or transmitted
by any means, electronic, mechanical, photocopying, recording,
or otherwise, without written permission from the publisher.
No patent liability is assumed with respect to the use
of the information contained herein. While every precaution
has been taken in the preparation of this book, the
publisher assumes no responsibility for errors or omissions.
Neither is any liability assumed for damages resulting
from the use of the information contained herein.

International Standard Book Number: 0-672-21614-0
Library of Congress Catalog Card Number: 79-63864

Printed in the United States of America.

Preface

This book was started in early 1977, when the two-volume set *Introductory Experiments in Digital Electronics and 8080A Microcomputer Programming Interfacing* was in the final stage of preparation. I had just begun a six-month study leave from the Canberra College of Advanced Education and had come to Blacksburg to work with the authors of the Blacksburg Continuing Education Series for three months. During my stay with the authors I was given some preliminary experiments that had been written about the Intel Corporation's 8255 Programmable Peripheral Interface (PPI) integrated circuit. After completing the experiments and reading the available information about the 8255 I was excited by the concept of a generalized software-programmable integrated circuit, so I suggested that I write the text for a book about the 8255 chip and expand and revise the experiments to make a general-purpose book, one that would appeal to students, experimenters, computer hobbyists, engineers, scientists, and other users of programmable interface chips.

In the very early stages of preparation, two important points emerged:

1. The various modes of operation of the PPI reflect the major parallel-data input/output techniques used with microcomputers.
2. The use of generalized software-configurable LSI integrated circuits, which concentrate microcomputer interface hardware, would increase. Flexibility is built in through designs that allow

the configuration of the devices to be changed through sending *control bytes* to a *control register* within the integrated circuits.

Hence the emphasis of the book was directed so that:

- The major microcomputer input/output techniques are introduced in Chapters 3 through 7, and then their implementation is illustrated through the use of the 8255 PPI.
- The procedure for configuring the PPI is introduced in a generalized way in Chapter 2 so that, once the procedure is mastered, it can be applied to other software-configurable (programmable) interface ICs with a minimum of difficulty. While the details of their application will change, the procedure for using them through access to their control and data (and possibly other) registers will remain essentially the same.

The reader is assumed to have mastered the basics of microcomputer programming and interfacing. This includes the topics of device select pulse generation, polled and vectored interrupts, accumulator and memory-mapped I/O, as well as assembly language programming. The topics of accumulator and memory-mapped I/O have been reviewed in Chapter 1 because of their importance in making the interface connections between the 8080A microprocessor chip or 8080A-based microcomputer and the 8255 chip.

For the details of microcomputer interfacing, the reader is referred to the two-volume set of books mentioned earlier. For details of microcomputer programming, you are referred to the two-volume set *8080/8085 Software Design*.

The experiments have been designed to reinforce the concepts in each chapter. The experiments assume some familiarity with digital electronics and solderless breadboarding. You will need some additional circuitry to perform the experiments. Useful digital breadboarding aids such as lamp monitors, pulsers, logic switches, and a clock are all used in the experiments. Some general SN7400-series integrated circuits are also required.

As with other books in the Blacksburg Continuing Education Series, this book has been designed to be self-instructional, and, to this end, answers to all of the questions in the experiments have been provided. Since your answers will probably agree with our observations, it may be tempting to move along quickly without a review of *why* the various observations were made, and what they are related to.

In laboratory-based classes where time is limited, there is a tendency to succumb to this temptation, without being aware of what is actually taking place in an experimental circuit. With care, these experiments can provide a very rewarding experience. We have also found that many of the more complex interface chips use techniques that are similar to those used in the 8255. Thus an understanding of the PPI chip will provide you with a head start when you are interested in using some of the latest interface chips.

The materials presented in this book have been tested with success in both formal laboratory class situations and in short-course presentations in which lectures and hands-on experience have been combined. Readers in Australia may get in touch with me directly for additional information.

This book would not have been completed without the help of many people. I am particularly indebted to Peter Rony, Dave Larsen, and Jon and Chris Titus for their helpful advice and encouragement throughout the preparation of this book. From the Canberra CAE, my thanks to Roberta Vetter and to Margaret Bonnett for the many hours spent carefully typing drafts and then the final manuscript; to Tony Howkins and John Houldsworth for diagram preparation; and to Steve Morland for artwork in Chapter 7 and the preparation of the final assembled programs.

Finally, my love and thanks to my wife, Anne, whose support, encouragement, patience, and understanding during the writing was so necessary and so readily forthcoming. I dedicate this book to her.

PAUL F. GOLDSBROUGH

Contents

1

Introduction to the 8255 PPI

1-1. SOME QUESTIONS AND ANSWERS

In books and magazines that discuss microcomputers, increasing mention is being made of the Programmable Peripheral Interface, or PPI. This device is being used extensively by original equipment manufacturers as an input/output integrated circuit in microcomputer-based products. It is also being used increasingly by electronics engineers, technicians, and hobbyists.

- What is it?
- Where does it fit as an element in a microcomputer system?
- Why use it?
- How do you use it?

These are questions which we will discuss in the following pages using the Intel 8255 Programmable Peripheral Interface Chip as an example.

The PPI is a 40-pin large-scale integrated-circuit (LSI) "chip" that is used in a microcomputer as an *interface* between the microcomputer data bus and external input/output devices. This broad description also applies to other input/output (I/O) chips, e.g., the programmable communications interface (8251), or USART. The PPI differs from the USART in that the PPI is designed for *parallel data transfer,* whereas the USART is used for serial data transmission.

While the details of their application in a microcomputer system are of course different, the basic approach to their use is the same. Hence, when you have completed this book and mastered the basic techniques involved in using the PPI, you will find understanding and applying the USART and other programmable input/output devices much easier. (Such devices include Motorola's 6820 Programmable Interface Adaptor (PIA) and 6850 Asynchronous Interface Adaptor (ACIA), Texas Instruments' TMS 6011 UART, and Intel's 8259 Interrupt Controller.)

Fig. 1-1 shows a block diagram of a typical Intel 8080-based microcomputer. This diagram illustrates the position of the PPI and its relationship to the other system components. For clarity, not all of the data, address, and control paths have been included. Notice that the PPI is connected to the microcomputer via the data bus and that it connects the microcomputer to the outside world via 24 I/O lines. These are generally divided into three 8-bit bytes, which are labelled PA0–PA7, PB0–PB7, and PC0–PC7.

There are two major advantages in using the PPI in a microcomputer system. The first is that the PPI concentrates parallel input/output operations into one integrated circuit, unless more than 24 input/output lines are required. Since all input/output logic is on one integrated circuit, both interfacing complexity and chip count are reduced, with a resulting reduction in cost. The second, and perhaps most important advantage of using the PPI, is the tremendous flexibility which it brings to microcomputer I/O interfacing. This flexibility is obtained by making the PPI *software configurable*—hence its name, the *programmable* peripheral interface. The configuration of its 24 I/O lines for input, output, or perhaps bidirectional I/O is then under *software,* rather than hardware control. This makes the allocation of I/O lines and any subsequent alterations much easier. If, for example, you wish to add an extra input or output device to your microcomputer system, or, if you decide to alter the type of peripheral you are using from perhaps a light display to a video display terminal, then all that is needed, apart from perhaps adding or removing one or two control lines in some cases, is to change your input/output software.

Simple in concept? The author thinks so, and it is simple in practice once you have an overview of the chip electronics and user procedures. This is our task in the coming chapters. We will begin first, though, with a review of basic input/output techniques. Before doing so, it is only fair in this introduction of the PPI to mention some of

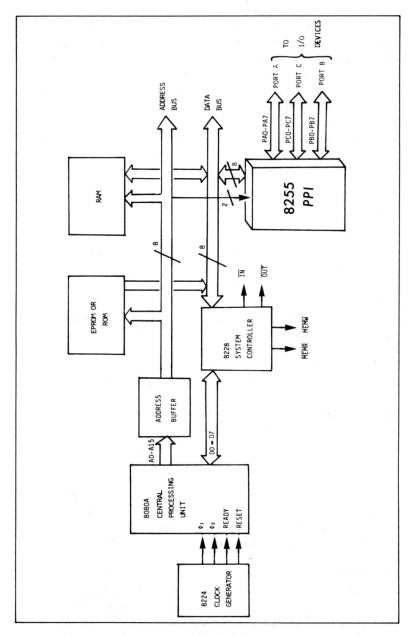

Fig. 1-1. A generalized 8080A-based microcomputer system showing the functional position of the Programmable Peripheral Interface.

its disadvantages. While it does concentrate the I/O lines in one area, this may not always be desirable. The software configuration of the device will also add, on average, approximately 10 bytes to the length of a program and this may cause the program to exceed say 1K bytes with the resultant need for a second ROM for program storage. Also, once the input/output interface requirements have been established, it may be less expensive to use standard I/O ports of the type to be described in the next section, even allowing for the additional costs in the layout of the printed-circuit board. Finally, the outputs of a PPI (8255) do not have the full fan-out of standard 7400-series integrated circuits.

1-2. INPUT/OUTPUT BASICS

The fundamental task of I/O transfers is to either transfer digital data from a register within the microcomputer to an external output device such as a teletypewriter, keyboard, another computer, light, relay, and so on, or to input digital data from an external device to the microcomputer. The digital data may be transferred in *serial* form, in which case a UART or USART may be used; or it may be transferred in *parallel* form. We will discuss only this latter class of I/O transfers here.

The transmission of parallel digital data or bytes of information to and from the microcomputer can be accomplished in either of two ways, both of which are associated with the internal registers of the microcomputer. Fig. 1-2 shows the seven registers which are available in the 8080A. These include six general-purpose registers (B, C, D, E, H and L) and the accumulator. The accumulator is a special register, as all arithmetic and logical operations are carried out with a data byte which is held in the accumulator. In general, when data bytes are input to or output from the accumulator, the input/output procedure is known as *accumulator I/O*. If the data byte is transferred directly between an external I/O device and a general-purpose register, the technique is known as *memory-mapped I/O*.

(A) Accumulator I/O

Accumulator I/O is the simplest input/output technique to understand and use. Only two special I/O instructions are needed for data transfer between the accumulator and an external device. The external device is assigned one of 256 device codes, which are encoded in an 8-bit device code. To input data, we use the instruction

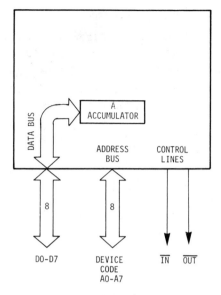

(A) Accumulator I/O.

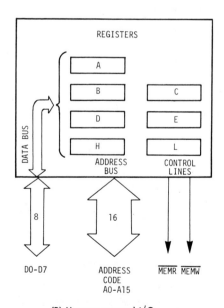

(B) Memory-mapped I/O.

Fig. 1-2. Schematic representations of accumulator and memory-mapped I/O.

where <B2> is the 8-bit device code of the input device. During the execution of this instruction, a control signal, $\overline{\text{IN}}$, is set to a logic low by the 8228 system controller chip (*cf* Fig. 1-1) when the device code byte <B2> appears on the address lines A0–A7. In 8080 systems the device code is also duplicated on address lines A8–A15. The IN pulse and the device code must then be used to generate a data transfer synchronizing pulse which is known as a *device select pulse*. One method of doing this is illustrated in Fig. 1-3. The device select pulse is then used to enable three-state buffers, which place the input data on the data bus, to be latched by the accumulator inside the 8080 microprocessor.

Outputting data with accumulator I/O is done in an analogous manner. The two-byte instruction

OUT
<B2>

is used, where <B2> is an 8-bit data byte that represents the device code of the device to which data is being output. This time, an $\overline{\text{OUT}}$ pulse is generated by the 8228 system controller (using 8080A status information) at the same time as the device code. A circuit such as that shown in Fig. 1-3 is again used to produce a device select pulse

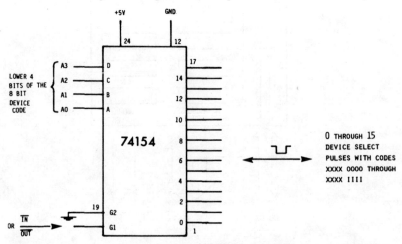

Fig. 1-3. Circuit used to generate accumulator I/O device select pulses. This is not an absolute decoder as only four of the eight address lines have been used for device address decoding.

which this time is used to latch the data byte appearing on the data bus from the accumulator. Figs. 1-4A and 1-4B show typical circuits for accumulator input and output respectively.

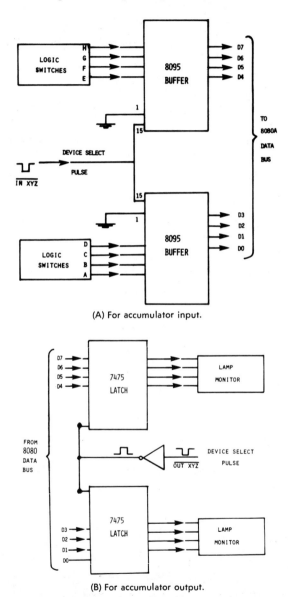

(A) For accumulator input.

(B) For accumulator output.

Fig. 1-4. Typical circuits for buffering accumulator I/O input data and latching output data.

The advantages of accumulator I/O are simplicity and directness of approach. The input or output of information requires the use of only the two special instructions provided. This is particularly advantageous when first using a microcomputer. There are two possible disadvantages to this I/O technique. The first and most important is that all data bytes being input or output must go via the accumulator. In many cases the origin of output data or the destination of input data is read/write memory or one of the general-purpose registers. This means that extra instructions will be required to shift the data bytes to or from the accumulator. The extra time and memory requirements may, in some circumstances, be critical. The second disadvantage is that only 256 device codes are available for input/output devices. The author honestly doubts whether this second point is really a serious problem for most users of microprocessors.

(B) Memory-Mapped I/O

The technique used in memory-mapped I/O is to trick the 8080A into thinking that the I/O device is, in fact, part of the memory. As the microprocessor has no real way of knowing what type of "memory" device it is accessing, all that is required is to:

- Use memory data transfer instructions in input/output subroutines.
  Examples of such instructions include:

MOV r, M	ADC M	CMP M
MOV M, r	SBB M	MVI M

  where
      r represents one of the seven 8080A registers,
      M is the memory location addressed indirectly by the contents of register pair H and L.

- Decode *address select pulses* using the address lines (A0–A15) and the memory read/write control signals, $\overline{\text{MEMR}}$ and $\overline{\text{MEMW}}$, to select or enable a three-state buffer (for input) or a latch (for output).

Proceeding in this way, 64K (1K = 1024) device codes become available. In practice, at least the first 32K addresses (address bit A15 at logic 0) are reserved for memory. If memory requirements are only moderate, the second half of memory, i.e., addresses above 32K, are allocated to memory I/O (address bit A15 to logic 1). This is illustrated in Fig. 1-5.

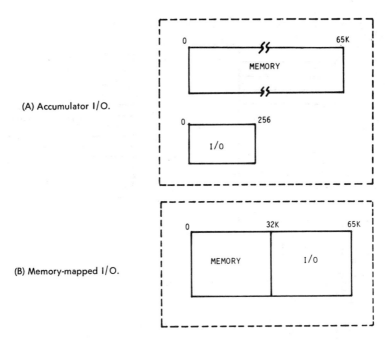

Fig. 1-5. Memory block comparison between accumulator I/O and memory-mapped I/O.

Usually, *absolute* or unique decoding of a 16-bit memory address is not required, and a circuit such as the one shown in Fig. 1-6, which employs *lineal* or single-line decoding, can be used if several device codes are required. If more than 32K of memory is needed, the I/O address allocations can be reduced to 16K, 8K, or 4K, etc., by gating address bits A15, A14, A13, respectively, together in place of the inverter shown in Fig. 1-6.

It is important to understand the concept of memory-mapped I/O since microprocessors, in general, do not have the special input and output instructions which are available in Intel microprocessors and which were described in the accumulator I/O technique earlier. The advantage of memory-mapped I/O is that all the general-purpose registers can be used for data transfers to and from peripherals. Logical operations can also be carried out directly between a byte in the accumulator and the contents of an input port (usually representing peripheral status information). In some cases this can result in an increase in overall system speed. However, memory-mapped I/O is much less efficient than accumulator I/O in terms of its memory requirements, as it ties up the H and L register pair (in an 8080-

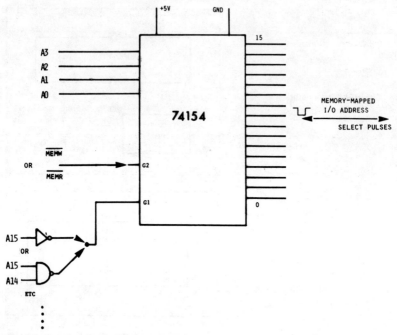

Fig. 1-6. Decoder circuit for the generation of 16 different memory I/O address select pulses. With the inverter and A15 in use the HI address byte is 200 and the LO address byte ranges from 000 to 017. Note that the addresses are neither unique nor absolute.

based microcomputer) for addressing plus one other register for data. In addition, memory-mapped I/O usually requires more complex decoding schemes than does accumulator I/O. The author has used both I/O techniques and prefers accumulator I/O for all but the most time-critical I/O tasks. In this book, examples of using both techniques for interfacing the PPI to the 8080 will be included.

To complete this brief discussion of the basic input/output techniques, Charts 1-1 and 1-2 summarize the important characteristics of accumulator and memory-mapped I/O. NOTE: For both memory-mapped I/O and accumulator I/O care should always be taken to ensure that the decoding of the memory address or device code address is sufficient to guarantee unique addresses for the input/output devices. The extent of this decoding depends simply on the size of the microcomputer-based system. In small systems the use of individual address lines (lineal decoding) will probably be adequate. Larger systems or systems likely to be expanded will require additional decoding.

Chart 1-1. Summary of Characteristics of Accumulator I/O

8080A instructions:	OUT <B2>
	IN <B2>
Control signals:	O̅U̅T̅
	I̅N̅
Data transfer:	Between accumulator and I/O device
Device decoding:	An 8-bit device code, A0 to A7 **or** A8 to A15, that is byte <B2> in the IN or OUT instruction.
Terminology:	The I/O processes are called **input** and **output**. The decoded signal that strobes an I/O device will be called a **device select pulse.**

Chart 1-2. Summary of Characteristics of Memory-Mapped I/O

8080A instructions:	MOV B,M	MOV M,H	ANA M
	MOV C,M	MOV M,L	XRA M
	MOV D,M	MOV M,A	ORA M
	MOV E,M	STAX B	CMP M
	MOV H,M	STAX D	INR M
	MOV L,M	LDAX B	DCR M
	MOV A,M	LDAX D	MVI M
	MOV M,B	ADD M	STA <B2> <B3>
	MOV M,C	ADC M	LDA <B2> <B3>
	MOV M,D	SUB M	SHLD <B2> <B3>
	MOV M,E	SBB M	LHLD <B2> <B3>
Control signals:	M̅E̅M̅R̅		
	M̅E̅M̅W̅		

Data transfer:	Between memory-mapped I/O device and registers B, C, D, E, H, L, or the accumulator (register A)
Device decoding:	A 16-bit device code, A0 to A15, that is contained either in register pair H; register pair B; register pair D; or is bytes <B2> and <B3> for the STA, LDA, SHLD, or LHLD instructions. In some instances it is useful and convenient to reserve the upper 32K memory area for memory-mapped I/O addresses; when A15 on the address bus is at logic 1, memory I/O exists. Bits A0 through A7 can be used to decode a specific I/O device when A15 = 1. The I/O device is made to look like an 8-bit memory location and the memory reference instructions are used in their normal manner to read from or write into the specific memory I/O device.
Terminology:	The memory-mapped I/O processes will be called **read** and **write** rather than input and output. The decoded signal that strobes a memory-mapped I/O device will be called an **address select pulse** rather than a device select pulse.

1-3. SUMMARY OF EXPERIMENTS 1-1 THROUGH 1-5

The objectives of the experiments are as follows:

Experiments 1-1 and 1-2: These two experiments will show you how to construct a simple bus monitor, a counting circuit, and a hardware single-step circuit. The circuits are used in later experiments and are provided for information if your 8080A-based microcomputer does not have them already wired.

Experiments 1-3 to 1-5: In these experiments the techniques of memory-mapped I/O and accumulator I/O are illustrated. If you are not familiar with these topics, you should do these experiments.

Experiment	*Description*
1-1	The purpose of this experiment is to wire a pair of circuits on an SK-10 socket that (a) count different types of synchronizing pulses, and (b) monitor the information present on the bidirectional data bus.
1-2	The purpose of this experiment is to construct a single-step circuit for an 8080A-based microcomputer.
1-3	In this experiment you will wire and examine the operation of the 8212 integrated-circuit chip as a memory-mapped input port.
1-4	The purpose of this experiment is to demonstrate the execution of an AND operation between a memory-mapped input port and the accumulator.
1-5	This experiment demonstrates and compares the behaviour of two I/O techniques, viz, accumulator and memory-mapped I/O, for the input of data into an 8080 microcomputer.

EXPERIMENT 1-1
BUS MONITOR AND COUNTING CIRCUITS

Purpose

The purpose of this experiment is to wire a pair of circuits on a solderless breadboarding socket that (a) count different types of synchronizing pulses, and (b) monitor the information present on the bidirectional data bus.

Pin Configuration of Integrated Circuits (Fig. 1-7)

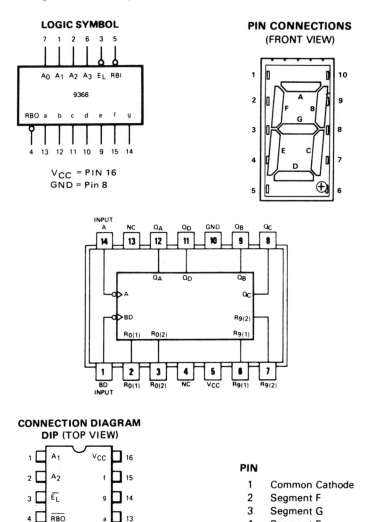

PIN

PIN	
1	Common Cathode
2	Segment F
3	Segment G
4	Segment E
5	Segment D
6	Common Cathode
7	Decimal Point
8	Segment C
9	Segment B
10	Segment A

Fig. 1-7. IC pin configurations.

Schematic Diagrams of Circuits (Fig. 1-8)

Counting Circuit—A Hewlett-Packard common-anode seven-segment display integrated circuit has been used in this configuration (Fig. 1-8A).

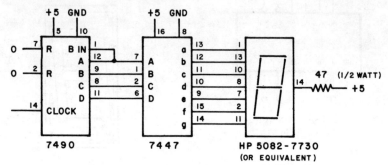

(A) Counting circuit.

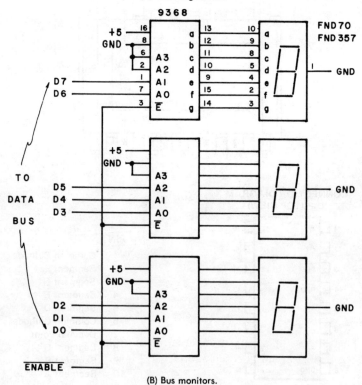

(B) Bus monitors.

Fig. 1-8. Schematic diagrams of circuits.

Bus Monitors—A Fairchild 9368 latch/decoder/driver integrated circuit has been used to drive the FND70 common-cathode seven-segment display chips (Fig. 1-8B). Pin outputs for one section have been shown, for purposes of clarity.

Step 1

Wire the counting circuit and one of the bus monitor circuits preferably on a single solderless breadboarding socket. You may wish to leave room for additional chips and/or displays for possible expansion of your circuits.

Step 2

In the space below, list the various types of synchronizing signals that you can count with the counting circuit given in Fig. 1-8A.

Signals such as $\overline{\text{MEMR}}$, $\overline{\text{MEMW}}$, $\overline{\text{IN}}$, $\overline{\text{OUT}}$, $\overline{\text{INT}}$ and other control bus signals can be counted.

Step 3

In the space below, explain the different types of inputs that can be applied to the latch inputs of the circuits in Fig. 1-8B. We shall call either of these circuits a *bus monitor* for the bidirectional data bus on the 8080 microprocessor chip.

You can latch input data, output data, memory read data, memory write data, and interrupt instruction vectors, provided the appropriate control line is applied to the latch enable input of the bus monitor circuit.

EXPERIMENT 1-2
SINGLE-STEP CIRCUIT

Purpose

The purpose of this experiment is to construct a single-step circuit for an 8080A-based microcomputer.

Pin Configuration of Integrated Circuit Chip (Fig. 1-9)

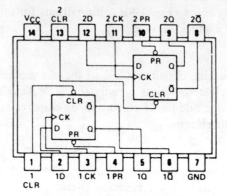

Fig. 1-9. Pin configuration of 7474.

Schematic Diagram of Circuit (Fig. 1-10)

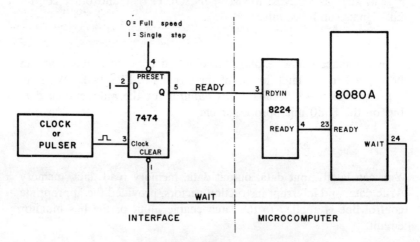

Fig. 1-10. Single-step circuit.

Program (Fig. 1-11)

```
                /
                /SINGLE STEP TEST PROGRAM
      :         /
                *003 000
003 000 000  START,  NOP     /NO OPERATION
003 001 074          INRA    /INCREMENT ACCUMULATOR BY ONE
003 002 323          OUT     /OUTPUT ACCUMULATOR CONTENTS
003 003 000          000     /DEVICE CODE OF OUTPUT PORT
003 004 303          JMP     /UNCONDITIONAL JUMP
003 005 000          START   /LO MEMORY ADDRESS OF JUMP
003 006 003          0       /HI MEMORY ADDRESS OF JUMP
```

Fig. 1-11. Program for single-step circuit.

Step 1

Wire the circuit shown in Fig. 1-10. If you are using a Mini-Micro Designer (MMD-1) microcomputer, the READY and WAIT lines may be found on the solderless breadboarding socket. Otherwise you will need to locate these control lines on your microcomputer. Connect your bus monitor circuit to the data bus, and connect the latch enable line to ground. The latches will now be permanently enabled and the bus monitor will continuously display the data appearing on the data bus.

Step 2

Enter the program in Fig. 1-11 into read/write memory.

Step 3

Begin execution of the program at the *full speed* of your micro-computer. What do you observe on the bus monitor? Why?

We observed that all the bus monitor LEDs were lit (8's on a seven-segment display). The reason for this is that the bus monitor is displaying machine instructions and data bytes as they appear on the data bus during program execution. At full microcomputer speed these bytes are changing so rapidly that the LEDs of the bus monitor appear permanently lit.

Step 4

To test that your single-step circuit is operating correctly, switch to *single step* and begin stepping through your program *one machine cycle* at a time by pressing your single-step push-button switch. Write down, in the space below, the bytes that you observe until a clear sequential pattern emerges. Using this data, together with observations of when the data byte at output port 0 appears, you should be able to deduce the machine cycle at which data from the accumulator is output to port 0.

The sequence of observed bytes was:

000, 074, 323, 000, ***, 303, 000, 003

where the *** byte represents the data byte being output from the accumulator. Its value changes as the program is executing.

EXPERIMENT 1-3
A MEMORY-MAPPED INPUT PORT

Purpose

The purpose of this experiment is to wire and examine the operation of the 8212 (SN74S412) integrated-circuit chip as a memory-mapped input port.

Pin Configuration and Truth Table for the 8212 Eight-Bit Input/ Output Port (Fig. 1-12)

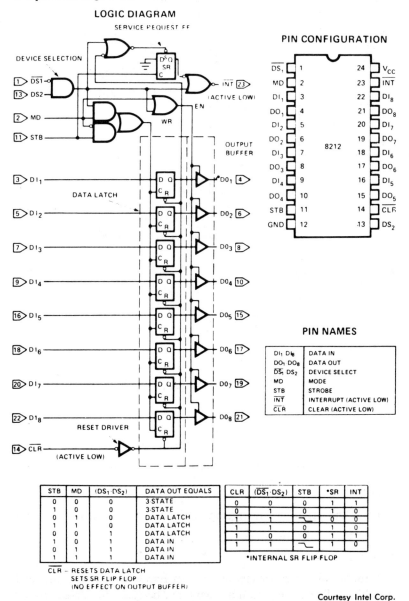

Courtesy Intel Corp.

Fig. 1-12. I/O port pin configuration and truth table.

Schematic Diagram of Circuit (Fig. 1-13)

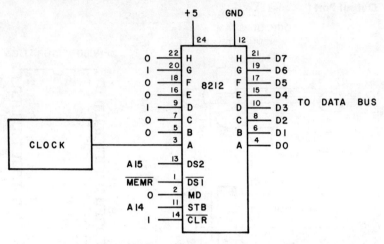

Fig. 1-13. 8212 IC as memory-mapped input port.

Program (Fig. 1-14)

```
                /
                /MEMORY MAPPED I/O TEST PROGRAM
                /
                DB BUSMON 000
                DW MMCODE 300 000
                *030 000
030 000 041           LXIH    /LOAD H,L WITH ADDRESS SELECT CODE
030 001 000           MMCODE  /LO ADDRESS BYTE
030 002 300           0       /HI ADDRESS BYTE
030 003 176  LOOP,    MOVAM   /LOAD A WITH CONTENTS OF
                               /LOCATION "M"
030 004 323           OUT     /OUTPUT A TO PORT 0
030 005 000           BUSMON  /DEVICE CODE FOR PORT 0
030 006 303           JMP     /JUMP TO LOOP AT
030 007 003           LOOP    /LO ADDRESS BYTE
030 010 030           0       /HI ADDRESS BYTE
```

Fig. 1-14. Program for memory-mapped input port.

Step 1

Load the program into memory. Enter 300_8 at memory address $003_8 002_8$.

Step 2

Wire the bus monitor circuit given in Experiment 1-1 in this unit. The block diagram for such a circuit will be given in subsequent experiments as shown in Fig. 1-15.

28

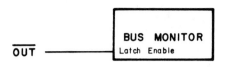

OUT ——————— BUS MONITOR / Latch Enable

Fig. 1-15. Diagram of bus monitor circuit.

Step 3

Wire the circuit given in Fig. 1-13. Fig. 1-16 is the application note for the use of the 8212 integrated circuit as a gated three-state input buffer.

The following shows the 8212 control pins, the control lines attached to these pins, and the logic levels required for data input:

8212 Input	$\overline{DS1}$	DS2	MD	STB	$\overline{CLR}$
Control Line	$\overline{MEMR}$	A15	0	A14	0
Logic Level for Data Input	0	1	0	1	1

Through reference to the application note (Fig. 1-16) and the truth table for the 8212 (Fig. 2-12), confirm for yourself that the five logic levels given above must be applied to the five 8212 control pins for data input. In the space below, write down the memory address re-

Gated Buffer (3 - STATE)

The simplest use of the 8212 is that of a gated buffer. By tying the mode signal low and the strobe input high, the data latch is acting as a straight through gate. The output buffers are then enabled from the device selection logic $\overline{DS1}$ and DS2. When the device selection logic is false, the outputs are 3-state.

When the device selection logic is true, the input data from the system is directly transferred to the output. The input data load is 250 micro amps. The output data can sink 15 milli amps. The minimum high output is 3.65 volts.

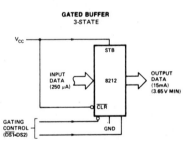

Fig. 1-16. Application note for the 8212.

quired to enable the 8212 for data input. Use an X for "don't care" bits.

If you replace your X bits by logic 0, is your memory address consistent with our address select code entered at LO address bytes 001_8 and 002_8 of the program entered at Step 1?

The memory address required to enable the 8212 for data input is

$$11\ XXX\ XXX_2\ XX\ XXX\ XXX_2$$

Replacing the "don't care" bits by logic 0 gives $300_8 000_8$, which is the address given at LO address bytes 001_8 and 002_8 in the program.

Step 4

Set the clock oscillator to about 10 Hz and execute your program at full microcomputer speed. What octal bytes do you observe on your bus monitor?

We observed the bytes 110_8 and 111_8, with the least significant octal digit changing at the same rate as the clock oscillator.

Step 5

Replace the HI address byte at memory location 003_8 002_8 in your program with the following bytes in turn: 010_8 and 365_8. Explain your observations of the behavior of the bus monitor during each program execution.

We observed normal data transfer from the input to the bus monitor with HI address byte 365_8 when the input port is enabled (A15 and A14 at logic 1). You observed 377_8 at the bus monitor when the program was executed with 010_8 at memory location 003_8 002_8. The address bit A15 is zero for this case, and so the 8212 input lines are in the three-state mode and no data is input.

Step 6

The bus monitor as wired in this experiment is being used as an output port. Is data transferred to this port using memory-mapped or accumulator I/O techniques? What is the disadvantage of this port as it presently stands?

The bus monitor is, of course, an accumulator output port since the OUT pulse is used to enable the latches during data output from the accumulator. The problem with the port as it presently stands is that it has no unique device code. You may wish to confirm this by changing "BUSMON" at LO memory location 005_8 in your program to another value. (NOTE: If you are using an MMD-1 microcomputer, do not use device codes 000_8, 001_8, or 002_8 since these are already used for the three LED output ports.)

Retain this circuit for the next experiment.

EXPERIMENT 1-4
EXECUTION OF AND OPERATION

Purpose

The purpose of this experiment is to demonstrate the execution of an AND operation between a memory-mapped input port and the accumulator.

Schematic Diagram of Circuit

Use the circuit wired in Experiment 1-3.

Program (Fig. 1-17)

```
              DB BUSMON 000
              *003 000
003 000 041          LXIH     /LOAD REGISTER PAIR H WITH:
003 001 003          003      /LO ADDRESS BYTE OF INPUT PORT
003 002 300          300      /HI ADDRESS BYTE OF INPUT PORT
003 003 076   TEST,  MVIA     /MOVE FOLLOWING BYTE IN ACCUMULATOR
003 004 001          001      /MASK BYTE
003 005 246          ANAM     /AND CONTENTS OF INPORT PORT
                              /WITH CONTENTS OF ACCUMULATOR
003 006 312          JZ       /IS RESULT ZERO? YES- JUMP BACK
003 007 003          TEST     /TO TEST
003 010 003          0
003 011 076          MVIA     /NO, FLAG BIT="1" SO LOAD A
003 012 377          377      /WITH ALL ONES
003 013 323          OUT      /OUTPUT BYTE
003 014 000          BUSMON   /TO PORT 0
003 015 166          HLT      /HALT THE MICROCOMPUTER
```

Fig. 1-17. Program for AND operation.

Step 1

Wire the memory-mapped input port circuit shown in Experiment 1-3 (Fig. 1-13) if it is not already wired on your breadboard.

Step 2

Load and execute the program of Fig. 1-17 with your clock oscillator set to about 2 Hz. What happens at output port BUSMON?

We observed the octal code 377 on the bus monitor.

Step 3

Alter the bytes at LO memory addresses 004 and 005 to 111 and 276. This latter byte is the op code for the CMP M instruction. Now execute the program at full speed. Note and explain in the space below what you observe on the bus monitor.

We observed 377 on the bus monitor. The CMP M instruction compares the contents of the accumulator (111 in this case) with the contents of memory location M (in this case the memory-mapped input port). If the two bytes are equal, the zero flag is set and the program loops to TEST. If the two bytes are not equal, a 377 is output to the bus monitor.

Questions

1. What is the advantage of memory-mapped I/O over accumulator I/O in this masking situation?

2. Write a program using accumulator I/O to replace the program given in this experiment. Compare the number of bytes required in each case.

EXPERIMENT 1-5
ACCUMULATOR I/O VERSUS MEMORY-MAPPED I/O

Purpose

The purpose of this experiment is to demonstrate and compare the behavior of two different I/O techniques, viz., *accumulator I/O* and *memory-mapped I/O,* for the input of data into an 8080 microcomputer.

Pin Configuration of Integrated Circuits (Fig. 1-18)

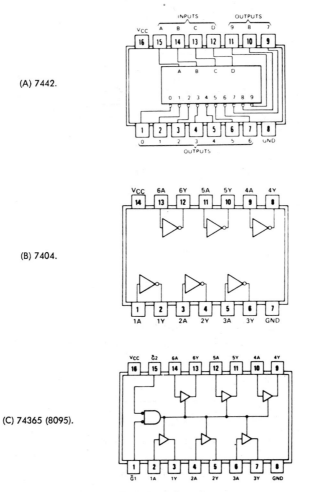

(A) 7442.

(B) 7404.

(C) 74365 (8095).

Fig. 1-18. IC pin configurations.

Schematic Diagrams of Circuits (Fig. 1-19)

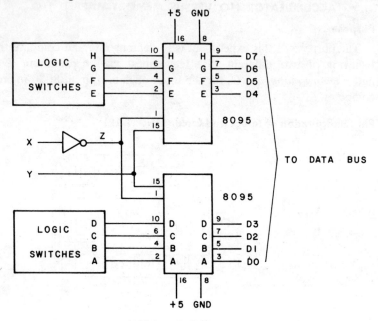

(A) Input buffer circuit.

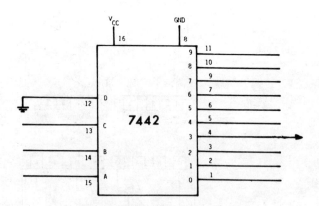

(B) Device select pulse decoder circuit.

Fig. 1-19. Circuit diagrams.

Program No. 1. Accumulator I/O (Fig. 1-20)

```
                DB BUFF 200
                *003 000
003 000 333   START,  IN      /INPUT DATA TO A FROM
003 001 200           BUFF    /BUFFER CIRCUIT
003 002 323           OUT     /OUTPUT THE DATA BYTE TO
003 003 000           000     /PORT 0
003 004 303           JMP     /UNCONDITIONAL JUMP TO
003 005 000           START   /LO MEMORY ADDRESS BYTE
003 006 003           0       /HI MEMORY ADDRESS BYTE
```

Fig. 1-20. Program No. 1

Program No. 2. Memory-Mapped I/O (Fig. 1-21)

```
                DW MMCODE 300 000
                *003 020
003 020 041           LXIH    /LOAD REGISTER PAIR H WITH:
003 021 000           MMCODE  /MEMORY MAPPED I/O DEVICE
003 022 300           0       /CODE
003 023 176   LOOP,   MOVAM   /MOVE CONTENTS OF MEMORY LOCATION M
                              /GIVEN BY REGISTER PAIR H INTO A
003 024 323           OUT     /OUTPUT THE CONTENTS OF A TO
003 025 000           000     /PORT 0
003 026 303           JMP     /JUMP TO
003 027 023           LOOP    /LO ADDRESS BYTE
003 030 003           0       /HI ADDRESS BYTE
```

Fig. 1-21. Program No. 2.

Accumulator I/O

Step 1

Wire the input buffer circuit shown in Fig. 1-19A. Connect the control line $\overline{\text{IN}}$ to point Y and wire point X to a logic 1.

Step 2

Load Program No. 1 into memory. Set the buffer circuit device code byte BUFF at memory location 003_8001_8 to 220_8.

Step 3

Run the program at full microcomputer speed. Alter the logic switches at the input to the buffer circuit and explain in the space below what you observe at port 0.

We observed that the byte displayed at port 0 was the same as that set on the logic switches.

Step 4

Alter the buffer circuit device code byte BUFF to 350_8. Run your program again. What do you observe when the logic switches are altered?

We observed that the byte displayed on the bus monitor was again the same as that set at the logic switches. Explain, in the space below, why the device code byte had no effect.

The reason is that for the circuit wired in Step 1, the buffer enable pulse is $\overline{\text{IN}}$, which is generated each time an IN <B2> instruction is executed. For the device code to enable the three-state buffers, either:

- one of the bits (A0–A7) of the device code byte <B2>, which appears on the address lines during an IN instruction, must be gated with $\overline{\text{IN}}$ to produce a *device select pulse* or
- several or all of A0–A7 should be decoded to generate a pulse which is again gated with $\overline{\text{IN}}$ to produce a device select pulse.

In this case a NOR gate is available within the 8095 chip, and we will use this gate.

Step 5

Disconnect the logic 1 connection from point X and wire point X at your input buffer circuit to address line A7. Referring to the pin configuration diagram for the 8095 and also to the input buffer circuit, it may be seen that we now have $\overline{\text{A7}}$ and $\overline{\text{IN}}$ NORed together. The result is a logic output to the three-state buffers which is normally low (high-impedance state) and which goes high (enabled) when both $\overline{\text{A7}}$ and $\overline{\text{IN}}$ are low. This latter condition only occurs during the third machine cycle of an IN <B2> instruction. Hence the device code for the input buffer circuit will be

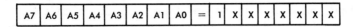

| A7 | A6 | A5 | A4 | A3 | A2 | A1 | A0 | = | 1 | X | X | X | X | X | X | X |

where X = "don't care."

Step 6

With BUFF at memory location $003_8 001_8$ set in turn to 100_8, 220_8, and 350_8, repeat Step 3 and explain why data is successfully transferred from the logic switches to output port 0 in the latter two cases but not in the first.

If you are having trouble with the answer to this question, review the comments in Step 5 and note which of the device codes in Step 6 has address bit A7 set to a logic 1.

Step 7

Clearly, considerable device code redundancy results from using a single address code bit to generate a device select pulse. Some or all of this redundancy may be removed by decoding some or all of the device code bits A0–A7 (or A8–A15). To illustrate this, disconnect power to your solderless breadboardirg socket and wire the SN7442 decoder circuit shown in Fig. 1-19B, preferably on the same solderle.s breadboarding socket as your input buffer circuit. Wire address lines A4, A3, and A2 to inputs C, B, and A, respectively, of the SN7442. Wire the SN7442 output "3" (pin 4) directly to point Z in the input buffer circuit and disconnect A7 from point X. Make sure that you also disconnect the inverter from Z. What device codes will now enable the input buffer circuit?

Any device code which has A4 equal to logic 0 and A3 and A2 both equal to logic 1 will enable the input buffer.

Step 8

Set BUFF to 00001111 = 017, repeat Step 4 and confirm that data is being successfully transferred from the logic switches to port 0 once you have applied power to your solderless breadboarding socket.

Memory-Mapped I/O

Step 9

To wire your input buffer circuit for memory-mapped I/O, remove power from your solderless breadboarding socket, disconnect $\overline{\text{IN}}$ from point Y in your circuit, and connect $\overline{\text{MEMR}}$ in its place. Also, disconnect the decoder output line from point Z, and connect address line A15 to point X. Remember also to reconnect the inverter to point Z. Address bit A15 will now determine whether the microcomputer is accessing memory (A15 is logic 0) or I/O devices (A15 is logic 1).

Step 10

Load program No. 2 into memory.

Step 11

Apply power to your solderless breadboarding socket and begin the execution of your program. While your program is running confirm that data which is input from the memory-mapped input port is displayed again at port 0.

Step 12

As for accumulator I/O, considerable device code duplication exists in this case when address bit A15 and $\overline{\text{MEMR}}$ are used, since any address above $200_8 000_8$ will enable the input buffer. Confirm that this is the case by substituting different address select codes at memory locations $003_8 021_8$ and $003_8 022_8$.

Step 13

A decoder circuit can again be used, as with accumulator I/O, to reduce this device code redundancy. Draw a circuit in the space below that would reserve addresses below 48K for memory, and addresses above 48K for I/O. You may want to test this circuit.

The required circuit shows A15 and A14 wired to the inputs of a two-input NAND gate which replaces the inverter at point Z in Fig. 1-19A.

Step 14

What if you desired to input an 8-bit byte from the logic switches into register C rather than the accumulator. What modifications would you need to make to the accumulator I/O and memory-mapped I/O programs to accomplish this objective? Write the new programs in the space below.

For the accumulator I/O program, a MOV C, A instruction would need to be added at location 003 002. For the memory-mapped I/O program, the MOV A, M instruction would be replaced by a MOV C, M.

Step 15

On the basis of these programs, identify one advantage and one disadvantage of memory-mapped I/O.

The advantage of memory-mapped I/O over accumulator I/O that is illustrated in these programs is that data can be moved directly into the desired register with memory-mapped I/O, whereas an extra MOV instruction is required with accumulator I/O. Where a large block of data is being transferred and processed, this saving of an instruction is useful. The disadvantage of memory-mapped I/O which is illustrated here is the longer length of the program and the need to tie up the H,L register pair for I/O.

2

An Overview of the 8255

2-1. ELECTRONICS

In this section we will examine the basic, functional electronic blocks within the PPI to see how these "blocks" interact with the outside world through their data and control lines. Our purpose is to examine the potential of the PPI as an I/O interface and also to see the hardware connections that are needed for satisfactory chip operation.

Fig. 2-1 shows a block diagram of the PPI. Notice that the PPI can be divided into three main units, *viz,* the interface circuitry to the 8080 central processing unit (CPU) module, a peripheral interface unit, and an internal control logic unit.

(A) Peripheral Interface Pins

Since over 50 percent of the pins of the 8255 are dedicated to data input or data output operations, we will look at these pins first. Data is transferred to and from external I/O devices through three 8-bit ports known as port A (PA0–PA7), port B (PB0–PB7), and port C (PC0–PC7).

The electronic characteristics and functions of these three ports are determined by the PPI operating mode, which is selected under program control. There are three main ways in which the 8255 I/O lines can be programmed:

- *Basic Input and Basic Output (Mode 0).* In this mode the 24 I/O lines are divided into two groups of eight lines each (ports

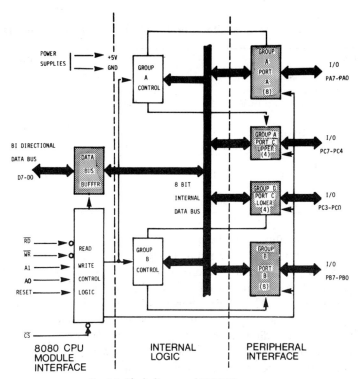

Fig. 2-1. Block diagram of 8255 PPI.

A and B) and two groups of four lines that together are called port C. Each port or group can then be individually programmed for *basic* input or output operation. In this operating mode, which is the simplest of the three, each assigned output port is latched. The input ports are not latched, operating as three-state input buffers.

- *Strobed Input and Strobed Output (Mode 1).* In this mode the PPI uses the two 8-bit ports, A and B, as unidirectional input or output ports. Each port transfers data in conjunction with a strobe or "handshaking" signal. Ports A and B use the 8 bits of port C to generate or accept these "handshaking" signals. Data is latched for both input and output at ports A and B.
- *Strobed Bidirectional I/O (Mode 2).* A single bidirectional I/O port (port A) is available for mode 2 operation. As with mode 1, strobing or "handshaking" is used to maintain an ordered flow of data to and from the cpu. Five bits of port C are used for this purpose.

Table 2-1. I/O Line Allocation for Mode 0, 1, and 2 Operations

Mode	Port A	Port B	Port C
0	BASIC INPUT/OUTPUT Outputs latched Inputs not latched	BASIC INPUT/OUTPUT Outputs latched Inputs not latched	BASIC INPUT/ OUTPUT Outputs latched Inputs not latched
1	STROBED I/O Inputs & Outputs latched	STROBED I/O Inputs & Outputs latched	CONTROL/STATUS BITS FOR PORTS A & B
2	STROBED BIDIRECTIONAL I/O Inputs & Outputs latched	—	CONTROL/STATUS BITS FOR PORT A

Table 2-1 summarizes the main ways in which the 24 I/O lines are allocated for these three major modes of operation.

When programming the operating mode for the PPI, you are not restricted to committing *all* of the PPI I/O lines to one particular operating role. The *mode control word,* which is used to define the operating mode for each of the PPI ports, is set up so each port can be assigned a different operating mode. If, for example, port A is programmed for mode 2 operation, the remaining eight lines of port B and three lines of port C can be configured for either mode 0 or mode 1 operation.

An additional feature of port C is that each bit may be individually set or reset. This is important since it permits strobe and gating signals to be generated by software using a *bit-set/reset control word.* This eliminates the need for additional external logic, although additional software steps will be required to generate the set/reset conditions.

(B) 8080A CPU Interface Pins

Referring to Fig. 2-1, there are eight data lines, six control lines, and two power supply lines which make up the remainder of the PPI chip pins. These pins are associated with the PPI's 8080 CPU interface (Fig. 2-1). Let us examine the function of each of these pins.

During the execution of the IN, OUT, and MOV input/output commands, the 8080 CPU communicates with the PPI via the microcomputer system data bus, which is connected to pins D0 to D7. All data bytes that pass between the 8080 and the 8255 are transmitted or received by a bidirectional 8-bit buffer. Now in any computer system there may be many devices, including read/write memories (RAMs), ROMs, EPROMs, PPIs, and USARTs, connected to the data bus. Since only one device at a time may be "active" if bus loading is to be avoided, the PPI, as with the other devices, has three-state data bus lines. These lines are enabled, and the chip is effectively connected to the bus, by a logic zero on the PPI *chip select* ($\overline{CS}$) line. A logic one on the chip select pin forces the PPI data bus lines into the high-impedance state. Once the PPI is enabled by a logic zero on $\overline{CS}$, the PPI must then be told whether it is to read data ($\overline{RD}$) from the I/O ports and place it on the data bus lines (D0–D7) to the 8080 or to write the data ($\overline{WR}$) which is present on the data bus lines (D0–D7) to the I/O ports. Clearly simultaneous logic zeros to $\overline{RD}$ and $\overline{WR}$ is an illegal condition!

Consider for a moment the types of byte which might be sent down the data bus to the PPI. These include:

- *Data bytes* for port A, port B, or port C.
- *Control bytes,* which are routed to a control register within the Read/Write Control Logic Block of the 8255. There are two types of control bytes: the *mode control word,* which specifies the operating modes of ports A to C, and the *bit set/reset control word,* which is used to set and reset the individual bits of port C.

When a data or control byte is sent to the PPI using accumulator or memory-mapped I/O, a *destination address* or code must also be sent at the same time to specify the byte type and its destination. The address pins A0 and A1 are used by the PPI for this purpose. Table 2-2

Table 2-2. Use of Address Pins A0 and A1

A_1	A_0	I/O Operation
0	0	DATA BUS ↔ port A
0	1	DATA BUS ↔ port B
1	0	DATA BUS ↔ port C
1	1	DATA BUS → control register

shows the way in which the signals that are connected to these pins define the type and destination of a byte being communicated between the 8080A and the 8255. Clearly these two address bits do not provide unique addressing when an 8-bit device code is available for accumulator I/O, or when a 16-bit address code is available for memory-mapped I/O. Suffice it to say for the moment that a non-unique address does not, in general, introduce difficulties.

The reset pin (RESET) is usually connected to the microcomputer's reset line. A logic 1 on this input clears all of the internal registers, including the control word register, and sets all of the I/O ports to their input mode. This latter feature can be useful for system initialization. Finally, the PPI requires a single +5-V supply (V_{cc} and GND) and this makes it easily adaptable to virtually all microcomputer systems.

(C) Internal Control Logic

As was mentioned earlier, the operating modes of ports A through C as well as the bit set/reset operation on port C are controlled by sending the PPI either a *mode* control byte or a *bit-set/reset* control byte under software control. The destination of this control word is the *control register* (within the read/write control logic block) whose code is A0 = 1, A1 = 1. The internal logic (Fig. 2-1) of the chip then manages the transfer of data and control information on the internal data bus. The mode control byte is transferred to two port controllers, which are designated GROUP A and GROUP B control. The GROUP A control module controls the mode definition of (and data transfer to and from) port A and the most significant four bits of port C. Similarly, the GROUP B control module supervises port B and the least significant four bits of port C.

The heart of the control logic, then, is the 8-bit control register since the control byte, which is written into this register, ultimately defines the operational characteristics of the PPI. Fig. 2-2 shows the formats of the two types of control byte. The most important point to note concerning the control word is that the most significant bit (D7) is used to specify the type of control word. If D7 is set to a logic 0 (Fig 2-2B), the control word will be used by the PPI to define the port C bit that is to be set or reset. If D7 is set to a logic 1 (Fig. 2-2A), the remaining control word bits will be used by the internal logic to specify the operating modes of each of ports A through C.

As an example of the use of the control word, let us assume that we require the PPI to be configured with:

PORT A:	Mode 0 Output	PORT C: BITS PC7–PC4	Mode 0 Input
PORT B:	Mode 1 Input	PORT C: BITS PC3–PC0	Mode 0 Output

Using Fig. 2-2A, the individual bits of the control word can be chosen as follows:

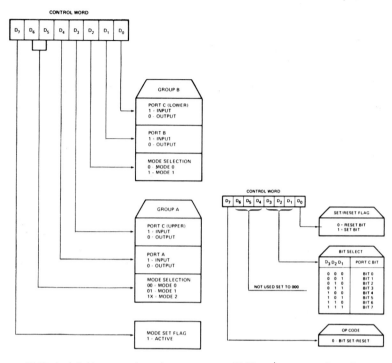

(A) Mode definition control word.   (B) Bit-set/reset control word.

Fig. 2-2. Comparison of the two types of the control word which defines the operational characteristics of the PPI.

D7	:	Opcode; mode set = 1
D6,D5	:	PORT A mode; mode 0 = 0,0
D4	:	PORT A I/O; output = 0
D3	:	PORT C upper I/O; input = 0
D2	:	PORT B mode; mode 1 = 1
D1	:	PORT B I/O; input = 1
D0	:	PORT C lower I/O; output = 0

Hence the mode control word would be:

$$1\ 0\ 0\ 0\ 0\ 1\ 1\ 0 = 206$$

In a similar manner a control word can be constructed from the table in Fig. 2-2B and sent, using an output instruction, to the control register to set or reset any of bits PC7 to PC0 of port C. To reset bit PC2, for example, the control word would be required. Note that a separate control word is needed to reset PC2, as only one bit set or reset operation can be accomplished with each bit-set/reset control word.

(D) Interfacing a PPI to a Microcomputer

Fig. 2-3 presents one approach to interfacing a PPI to an 8080-based microcomputer data bus for accumulator I/O. Notice that the chip select pin $\overline{CS}$ is connected to A7 through an inverter. The 8255 is then enabled when address line A7 is a logic high ($\overline{CS}$ low). The device-select address code format for the example in Fig. 2-3 is illustrated in Fig. 2-4. The addresses form the second byte of the IN and OUT instructions used to access the PPI in this example. Since there are so many "don't care" bits, considerable ambiguity of addressing exists, and so care is required to avoid enabling the PPI and another I/O peripheral on the data bus at the same time. The loading of the data bus that results will usually render the microcomputer inoperative and may damage the 8080.

The technique of using a single bit to enable a peripheral is known as *lineal device selection*. It is used in small systems, such as the Intel SDK-80, where the number of peripherals is small and the risks and problems, as explained above, are low. In bigger systems, such as the Intel SBC-80/10, absolute decoding of the chip select is used to

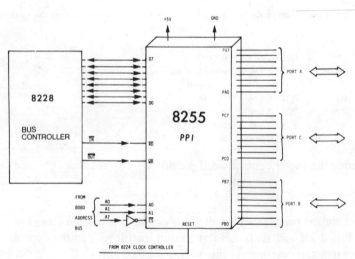

Fig. 2-3. Typical wiring diagram for 8255 PPI for accumulator I/O.

eliminate nonunique device addressing. The author recommends this even in small systems since small systems have a habit of growing! A 74154, four-line to 16-line decoder is usually quite adequate to decode address lines A7, A6, A5, and A4 and to provide a more unique chip select pulse, $\overline{\text{CS}}$.

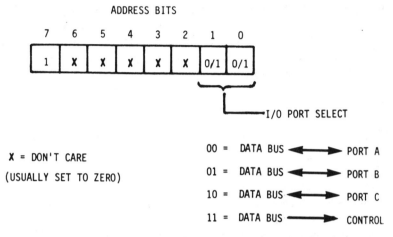

Fig. 2-4. Device-select address code format for the circuit of Fig. 2-3.

To interface the PPI in Fig. 2-3 for memory-mapped I/O, the following simple alterations must be made to the circuit:

- Replace the $\overline{\text{IN}}$ and $\overline{\text{OUT}}$ control signals with the memory-mapped I/O read and write control signals, $\overline{\text{MEMR}}$ and $\overline{\text{MEMW}}$, respectively
- Replace A7 with A15 to ensure that the addresses of the PPI, as a memory-mapped I/O port, are in the second half of memory.

2-2. STEPS FOR USING THE 8255

In the introduction we saw where the PPI fits in a microcomputer system and the reason for its popularity, *viz*, the ability to *program* the way it will look and behave to the outside world. As with most aspects of microcomputer usage, the application of this device in a microcomputer system requires a mix of hardware and software skills. The three main steps required to use a PPI are:

- Interface the PPI to the microcomputer using either accumulator or memory-mapped I/O.

- Program the operational mode of the 8255.
- Input or output data under software control.

In the previous section on the chip electronics, we saw how the PPI could be wired onto the 8080A data bus for accumulator I/O (*cf* Fig. 2-3). The method for constructing control word bytes to specify the operational mode of the PPI was also explained [Section 2-1(C)]. What remains, then, is to discuss, in broad terms, the software requirements of the PPI. The chapters that follow will then discuss in detail the electronics and programming required for the three operational modes of the PPI.

2-3. SOFTWARE

Regardless of the operational modes selected for the PPI I/O ports, the first step required of any program is a *system initialization subroutine*. In the simplest case this may contain steps for outputting, to the PPI, the mode control word required to specify the operating modes of the three I/O ports. As an example let us use the PPI, connected as shown in Fig. 2-3, with the operating modes of ports A through C specified as shown in the example in Section 2-1(C). Referring to that section, the required mode control word was 206. For the PPI in Fig. 2-3 the device address for the control register can be determined from Fig. 2-4. If we set the "don't care" bits, D2 through D6, equal to logic 0, the device address for the control register is:

$$1\ 0\ 0\ 0\ 0\ 0\ 1\ 1 = 203$$

Hence a simple PPI initialization subroutine, INT, could be as shown in Program 2-1.

```
            /
            /PPI  INITILISATION  SUBROUTINE:INIT
            /
            DB MODE 206
            DB CNTRL 203
            *003 200
003 200 365 INIT,   PUSHPSW /STORE PROCESSOR STATUS
003 201 076         MVIA    /LOAD A WITH THE FOLLOWING
003 202 206         MODE    /MODE CONTROL BYTE
003 203 323         OUT     /OUTPUT CONTROL BYTE TO
003 204 203         CNTRL   /CONTROL REGISTER
003 205 361         POPPSW  /RESTORE PROCESSOR STATUS
003 206 311         RET
```

Fig. 2-5. Program 2-1.

Program 2-1 (Fig. 2-5)

In mode 1 and mode 2 I/O operations and in certain mode 0 I/O operations, some of the bits of port **C** must be set using the bit-set/reset control word prior to using the PPI. In these cases the required

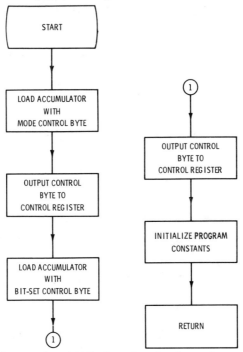

Fig. 2-6. Flow diagram of an initialization subroutine for a microcomputer containing a PPI.

bit-set/reset control word must also be sent to the PPI control register during system initialization. The generalized flow diagram of an initialization routine, shown in Fig. 2, illustrates the position within the subroutine of the required bit-set instructions.

Program 2-2 in Fig 2-7 shows a typical PPI initialization subroutine. Note that for short programs the PPI initialization coding could (and most probably would) be incorporated in the main program by omitting the PUSH, POP, and RETURN instructions.

Program 2-2 (Fig. 2-7)

Having initialized the PPI through the use of software, the next step is to transfer data through the PPI. In the case of the PPI in Fig. 2-3, interfaced for accumulator I/O, data may be input from any port or output to any port for basic mode 0 I/O using the following accumulator I/O instructions:

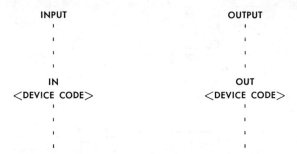

where the <device code> byte is the device address of ports A through C, as required. For the circuit in Fig. 2-3, for example, the

```
          /
          /SUBROUTINE: INITB
          /
          DB MODE 206
          DB CNTRL 203
          DB BITSET 005
          *003 100
003 100 365   INITB,  PUSHPSW /STORE PROCESSOR STATUS
003 101 076           MVIA    /LOAD ACCUMULATOR WITH THE
003 102 206           MODE    /FOLLOWING MODE CONTROL WORD
003 103 323           OUT     /OUTPUT MODE CONTROL WORD TO THE
003 104 203           CNTRL   /CONTROL REGISTER
003 105 076           MVIA    /LOAD ACCUMULATOR WITH
003 106 005           BITSET  /BIT SET/RESET CONTROL WORD
003 107 323           OUT     /OUTPUT IT TO THE
003 110 203           CNTRL   /CONTROL REGISTER
003 111 361           POPPSW  /RESTORE PROCESSOR STATUS
003 112 311           RET
```

Fig. 2-7. Program 2-2.

device addresses for ports A through C are given from Fig. 2-4 as 200_8, 201_8, and 202_8, respectively.

In mode 1 and 2 operation, data transfer is usually accompanied by the issue of and checking of *handshaking pulses* which are used to synchronize data transfer between an external interface and the PPI. The PPI is first checked to see if it is either READY to receive data

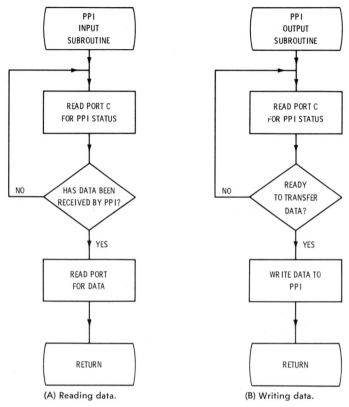

(A) Reading data.   (B) Writing data.

Fig. 2-8. Data transfer flow diagrams.

from the CPU for output or if it has received new data for input to the CPU. The lines of port C are used as status signals for ports A and B during mode 1 operation. They must then be checked by reading port C *prior* to inputting or outputting data through the PPI. The details of these software operations will be discussed in later chapters on mode 1 and mode 2 operation. The flow diagrams in Fig. 2-8 give an overview of the techniques involved.

3

Mode 0 Operation: Simple I/O

3-1. INTRODUCTION

In the following chapters we will examine in detail the three operating modes of the 8255. Modes 0 and 1 of the PPI reflect, in particular, two different *programmed data transfer* techniques, namely, *unconditional* and *conditional* data transfers. Let us begin by defining and discussing these terms. Superscripts in brackets refer to references in Section 3-6.

- *Programmed data transfer*[1]: A data transfer between a microcomputer system and external logic that is completely controlled by a microcomputer program. The majority of microcomputer input/output operations are programmed data transfers. This type of data transfer will not support high rates of data transfer because of the relatively slow instruction execution time for most microcomputers (at least 2 μs for the 8080A) and the need to execute a number of instructions in the process of inputting or outputting a data byte. For the improved data transfer rates, input/output operations between memory and an external device can be achieved without program intervention using the direct memory access technique. This technique is rarely used in microcomputer systems except perhaps in the interfacing of floppy-disc devices.
- *Unconditional data transfer*[3]: This is the simplest type of data transfer and assumes that the external device is always available

and ready for communication with the microcomputer. It is open-loop in nature as there is no feedback from the peripheral to inform the microprocessor that the peripheral is ready to receive data or that data is available on the data bus from the peripheral. The technique has also been described as simple I/O[1] to reflect its low level of difficulty in both programming and interfacing. It has also been described as *synchronous I/O*[2], presumably to reflect the fact that the data is transferred in synchronization with the microcomputer clock and without reference to the peripheral's state of readiness. However, the author feels that this well accepted and understood digital logic term is not applicable to microcomputer-controlled parallel data transfers, and only adds confusion. It can equally well be argued that because there is no *common* clocking of both the microprocessor and the I/O logic, the simple or unconditional I/O technique is *asynchronous*. To avoid confusion we will use either "simple I/O" or "unconditional I/O" to describe this I/O technique.

- *Conditional data transfer*[3]: In this approach, which is often called *handshaking I/O* and is very common in microcomputer systems, data is only transferred to or from a peripheral if it is ready for the transfer. This status information, in the form of logic flag bits, is provided by the peripheral. This technique could also be described as *asynchronous handshaking I/O*.

The mode 0 PPI operation, which we will discuss in this chapter, is designed for *unconditional* data transfers. When the 8255 is programmed for mode 0, the three 8-bit ports—port A, port B, and port C—are all available for this simple data transfer technique. It is most generally used in situations where a peripheral does not need to indicate to the microcomputer that it is ready to receive data, or that it has data available for input. A typical example of such a situation is the outputting of processed data by the microcomputer to various front-panel alphanumeric displays. In such cases data may be continuously altered without reference to the display. For input, there are again many cases where data may be input to the microcomputer without the need to monitor the status of the input peripheral. The 8 bits of an A/D converter which is continuously digitizing an analog input signal could be input to the microcomputer using simple or unconditional I/O. The outputs from SN7493, divide-by-16 counters, operating as event counters, could likewise be input in this way.

The discussion of accumulator I/O and memory-mapped I/O in Chapter 1 was based on the unconditional data transfer technique since in fact no mention of peripheral status information was made. Referring to Fig. 1-4, it will be seen that for input, the essential elements of the circuit (Fig. 1-4A) are the logic switches representing the peripheral and the two 4-bit three-state buffers. Clearly the logic switches would in practice be replaced by 7493 counters or an A/D converter, etc. The three-state buffer, however, is essential. For output the latches are also essential to ensure that the data that is output during a synchronous output operation is held until updated by the next output operation. In accordance with these requirements of simple I/O, all three PPI ports, when configured for mode 0 operation, have *latched outputs*. For mode 0 input the eight lines of each port are not "connected" to the microcomputer data bus until the port is addressed by the microcomputer for data input. Data is not latched by the PPI when mode 0 input is used, since it is transferred immediately through the PPI to the microcomputer. Fig. 3-1 shows how the simple I/O input and output circuits of Fig. 1-4A and 1-4B can be replaced by a single PPI. Note that the eight bits of port C are still available for additional unconditional data transfer tasks.

3-2. REQUIREMENTS

To use the PPI in its mode 0 configuration for unconditional or simple[3] I/O, the following steps (*cf* Section 2-2) are required:

(a) Program the PPI for mode 0 operation: This is the system initialization.
(b) Input and/or output data using simple I/O.

These steps then require the determination of:

- The mode control word for mode 0 input or output operation of ports A through C.
- The device code of the control register.
- The device addresses of ports A through C.

As an example, let us look at the circuit in Fig. 3-1 where port A has been configured for mode 0 output and port B has been configured for mode 0 input. Although port C is not used, we will assign it for mode 0 output. Referring then to Fig. 2-2A, bits D7 through D0 in the mode control word must be set as follows:

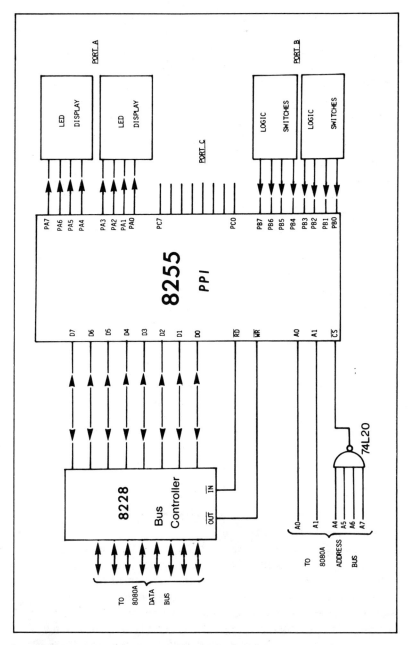

Fig. 3-1. The PPI is wired in this circuit for simple I/O (mode 0) to input data from port B and output data to port A.

D7	:	opcode; mode set = 1
D6,D5	:	group A mode selection; mode 0 = 0,0
D4	:	port A I/O: output = 0
D3	:	port C upper I/O; output = 0
D2	:	group B mode selection: mode 0 = 0
D1	:	port B I/O; input = 1
D0	:	port C lower I/O; output = 0

OR

D7,D6,D5,D4,D3,D2,D1,D0

1 0 0 0 0 0 1 0

202

Hence the required mode control word is 202_8. As an aside, note that we could have split port C into two sets of four bits, namely, port C upper (PC7–PC4) and port C lower (PC3–PC0); and assigned each of these independently for either simple input or output. This feature of port C is illustrated in Steps 8 through 10 of Experiment 3-1.

The device addresses for ports A through C and for the control register are determined, in general, by the address lines that are connected to the A0, A1, and $\overline{CS}$. In the circuit that is given in Fig. 3-1, the microcomputer's address lines A0 and A1 have been connected to the PPI's pins A0 and A1 as is usually the case. Address lines A4

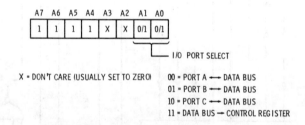

Fig. 3-2. Device-select address code format.

through A7 have to be NANDed together to provide a partially decoded chip select line for the $\overline{CS}$ input. The partial decoding used in this example is superior to the lineal device selection technique used in Fig. 2-3. Remembering that the chip select line is *active when set to a logic low,* and keeping in mind the function of pins A0 and A1, as summarized in Table 2-2, a device-select address code format can be generated for the above circuit as shown in the diagram of Fig. 3-2.

From the information in Fig. 3-2 and by setting the "don't care" bits to logic zero, it can be seen that the device codes for ports A through C and for the control register are:

PORT A: 360_8 PORT C: 362_8
PORT B: 361_8 CONTROL REGISTER: 363_8

As a general principle, after interfacing your PPI to the microcomputer, you should construct a diagram showing the device-select address code format for the circuit. Such a diagram is extremely useful, since it is a characteristic of the PPI circuit and can be used to obtain the appropriate address codes for configuring the PPI and accessing its ports for as long as the PPI circuitry remains unchanged.

3-3. PROGRAMMING

Having determined the mode control word which will configure the PPI ports for mode 0 input or output, and knowing the device codes for the ports and for the control register, the programming required then becomes a relatively simple matter. Fig. 3-3 shows a flowchart of a simple program which inputs data from port B in Fig. 3-1 and outputs results after processing to the LED displays at port A.

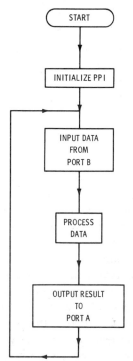

Fig. 3-3. Flowchart for mode 0 (simple) I/O.

A typical mode 0, simple I/O program for this flowchart is Program 3-1.

Program 3-1 (Fig. 3-4)

Note how, in this program, the mode control word and the device code for the control register were used for system initialization, and how the device codes for ports A and B were used for output and input, respectively.

```
            /MODE 0, SIMPLE I/O PROGRAM EXAMPLE
            /
            DB MODE 202
            DB PORTA 360
            DB PORTB 361
            DB CNTRL 363
            *000 000
000 000 076         MVIA      /LOAD A WITH:
000 001 202         MODE      /MODE CONTROL BYTE
000 002 323         OUT       /OUTPUT MODE CONTROL WORD TO
000 003 363         CNTRL     /CONTROL REGISTER
000 004 333  LOOP,  IN        /INPUT DATA FROM PORT B
000 005 361         PORTB     /PORT B DEVICE CODE
            /        .
            /        .
            /        - DATA PROCESSING -
            /        .
            /        .
            *000 070
000 070 323         OUT       /OUTPUT RESULTS IN ACCUMULATOR
000 071 360         PORTA     /TO PORT A
000 072 303         JMP       /JUMP TO INPUT NEW DATA
000 073 004         LOOP      /LO ADDRESS BYTE
000 074 000         0         /HI ADDRESS BYTE
```

Fig. 3-4. Program 3-1.

3-4. TIMING DIAGRAM

Fig. 3-5 shows a typical timing diagram for mode 0 input and output. The diagram represents the logic changes at the $\overline{\text{RD}}$, $\overline{\text{WR}}$, and D0–D7 inputs of the PPI during the execution of the program steps between memory locations $000_8 004_8$ and $000_8 071_8$ in the mode 0, simple I/O program given in Fig. 3-4.

The important point to note with simple I/O is that *data transfer occurs immediately upon receipt of a logic low signal at the $\overline{\text{RD}}$ or $\overline{\text{WR}}$ inputs of the PPI,* regardless of whether the data is fixed or changing and regardless of the readiness of the peripherals. For input, data is passed from the port currently being addressed through the PPI to the microcomputer when the $\overline{\text{RD}}$ line goes to logic low. Similarly, a logic low on the $\overline{\text{WR}}$ line will cause whatever data is present

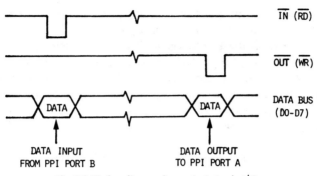

IN (RD)

OUT (WR)

DATA BUS
(D0-D7)

DATA INPUT
FROM PPI PORT B

DATA OUTPUT
TO PPI PORT A

Fig. 3-5. Timing diagram for mode 0 simple I/O.

on the microcomputer data bus to be *immediately latched* by the PPI port currently addressed. For accumulator I/O this is, of course, the contents of the A register (accumulator).

3-5. PORT C 4-BIT SUBPORTS

In a previous section of this chapter it was mentioned that bits D3 and D0 of the mode control word could be used to separately allocate port C upper (bits PC7–PC4) and port C lower (bits PC3–PC0) for mode 0 input or output, respectively (*cf* Fig. 2-2A). Hence, port C can be effectively divided into two 4-bit subports for mode 0 I/O as shown in Fig. 3-6.

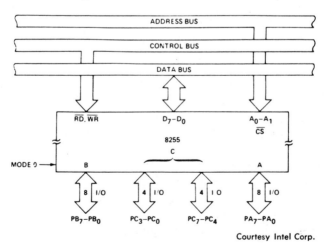

Courtesy Intel Corp.

Fig. 3-6. Schematic diagram of the grouping of interface lines available with the 8255 for mode 0 simple I/O.

While the 8 bits of port C can be assigned as two 4-bit I/O ports, these subports *cannot be independently accessed.* Communication of data to and from the PPI is via 8-bit bytes. Therefore, when using either port C upper or port C lower, care must be exercised at all times to ensure that the contents of one port C subport are not accidentally altered when writing data to the other subport. Table 3-1 illustrates the six likely conditions under which the two subports of port C might be accessed.

Table 3-1. Port C Subport I/O Allocation

Task	Port C Upper	Port C Lower	Requirement
Input	Input	Output	Mask out the 4
Input	Output	Input	bits not
Input	Input	Input	required
Output	Input	Output	Data set in lower 4 bits
Output	Output	Input	Data set in upper 4 bits
Output	Output	Output	Data set in upper and lower 4 bits

For data input from a port C subport, a masking technique is used to retrieve the required four bits. Thus, having determined from which subport data is required, an input instruction is used to input the 8 bits of port C. An 8-bit mask is then used to mask out the unwanted 4 bits. If the four bits of port C upper are required, four RAR (rotate right through carry) instructions may be needed to shift these bits into the four least significant bit positions if, for example, the 4 bits represent a bcd number or perhaps the least significant 4 bits of an event counter. Program 3-2 illustrates the program steps required to input data from port C upper using the circuit in Fig. 3-1. Note that the mode control word for PPI initialization has been altered to 212. Bit D3 in the mode control word has been changed from zero to one to redefine port C upper for input.

Program 3-2. Reading From Port C Upper (Fig. 3-7)

For data output to either port C upper or port C lower, data is simply placed in the appropriate 4 bits of the accumulator and the accumulator contents output to port C. The contents of the other 4 bits of the accumulator (i.e., the top four bits if data is being output to port C lower) are unimportant *as long as the remaining subport is programmed for input.* If, however, the remaining subport is also

```
                    /
                    /PORT C INPUT PROGRAM
                    /
                    DB MODE 212
                    DB PORTC 362
                    DB CNTRL 363
                    *001 000
001 000 076         MVIA        /LOAD A WITH MODE CONTROL
001 001 212         MODE        /WORD WHICH FOLLOWS
001 002 323         OUT         /OUTPUT MODE CONTROL WORD TO
001 003 363         CNTRL       /CONTROL REGISTER, FOR PPI INITIALIZATION
001 004 333         IN          /INPUT DATA FROM PORT C
001 005 362         PORTC       /PORT C DEVICE CODE
001 006 346         ANI         /MASK OUT THE BOTTOM FOUR BITS
001 007 360         360         /MASK BYTE
001 010 037         RAR         /ROTATE A RIGHT THROUGH CARRY
001 011 037         RAR         /ROTATE A RIGHT THROUGH CARRY
001 012 037         RAR         /ROTATE A RIGHT THROUGH CARRY
001 013 037         RAR         /ROTATE A RIGHT THROUGH CARRY
001 014 166         HLT         /HALT
```

Fig. 3-7. Program 3-2.

programmed for output, care must be taken to ensure that the 4 bits associated with this subport are not accidentally changed by an output operation to the intended half of port C. This is done by ensuring that the byte which is output to port C consists of the new 4-bit nibble for the subport which is being updated together with the previously output 4-bit nibble for the other subport. These values would probably be saved in a general-purpose register or in a read/write memory location. Program 3-3 (Fig. 3-8) illustrates the technique for outputting data to port C lower when output data is also latched at port C upper. We will assume that the PPI has already been initialized with both port C upper and lower configured for output.

Program 3-3. Writing to Port C Lower (Fig. 3-8)

```
                    DB PORTC 362
                    *020 000
                    /        .
                    /        .
                    /        .
020 000 006         MVIB        /LOAD REGISTER B WITH DATA
020 001 010         010         /FOR PORT C LOWER
020 002 016         MVIC        /LOAD REGISTER C WITH DATA
020 003 200         200         /FOR PORT C UPPER
020 004 171         MOVAC       /MOVE PORT C UPPER DATA TO A
020 005 346         ANI         /CLEAR LOWER FOUR BITS
020 006 360         360
020 007 260         ORAB        /OR IN DATA FOR PORT C LOWER
020 010 323         OUT         /OUTPUT DATA BYTE TO
020 011 362         PORTC       /PORT C
                    /        .
                    /        .
                    /        .
```

Fig. 3-8. Program 3-3.

3-6. REFERENCES

[1] Osborne, Adam *An Introduction to Microcomputers,* Adam Osborne and Associates, Inc., Berkeley, CA, 1976.

[2] Hilburn, J. L. & Julich, P. M. *Microcomputers/Microprocessors: Hardware, Software and Applications,* Prentice-Hall, Englewood Cliffs, 1976.

[3] Soucek, B. *Microprocessors & Microcomputers,* J. Wiley & Sons, New York, 1976.

8255 BLOCK DIAGRAM

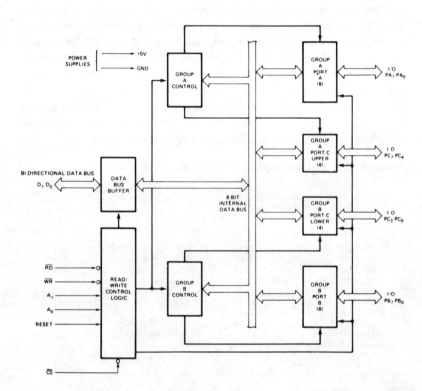

Fig. 3-9. IC block diagrams

3-7. SUMMARY OF EXPERIMENTS 3-1 THROUGH 3-3

Experiment	*Description*

3-1   (a) To interface the 8255 PPI for simple accumulator I/O.

        (b) To illustrate the use of the 8255 PPI in *mode 0 operation* for *data output*.

3-2   To illustrate the use of the 8255 PPI in *mode 0 operation* for *data input*.

3-3   The purpose of this experiment is to illustrate the mode 0 operation of the 8255 for combined input and output. The experiment is a synthesis of the procedures illustrated individually in Experiments 3-1 and 3-2 and so can be treated as

Pin Configuration and Block Diagram for Integrated Circuit (Fig. 3-9)

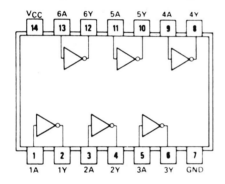

PIN CONFIGURATION

PIN NAMES

$D_7 - D_0$	DATA BUS (BI-DIRECTIONAL)
RESET	RESET INPUT
$\overline{CS}$	CHIP SELECT
$\overline{RD}$	READ INPUT
$\overline{WR}$	WRITE INPUT
A0, A1	PORT ADDRESS
PA7-PA0	PORT A (BIT)
PB7-PB0	PORT B (BIT)
PC7-PC0	PORT C (BIT)
V_{CC}	+5 VOLTS
GND	0 VOLTS

and pin configurations.

a hardware and software test of your understanding of mode 0 PPI operation.

EXPERIMENT 3-1
MODE 0 DATA OUTPUT OPERATION

Purpose

The aims of this experiment are the following:
(a) To interface the 8255 integrated-circuit chip for simple accumulator I/O operation.

Program (Fig. 3-10)

```
/
/PPI MODE 0 OUTPUT PROGRAM
/
          DB MODE 200
          DB DATA 200
          DB CNTRL 203
          *003 000
003 000 061        LXISP   /LOAD THE STACK POINTER WITH
003 001 200        200     /LO ADDRESS BYTE
003 002 003        003     /HI ADDRESS BYTE
003 003 076        MVIA    /MOVE INTO THE ACCUMULATOR THE
003 004 200        MODE    /MODE 0 CONTROL BYTE
003 005 323        OUT     /OUTPUT CONTENTS OF A TO
003 006 203        CNTRL   /CONTROL REGISTER
003 007 323  LOOP, OUT     /OUTPUT CONTENTS OF A TO
003 010 200        DATA    /PORT A.
003 011 074        INRA    /INCREMENT A
003 012 315        CALL    /CALL THE SUBROUTINE "DELAY"
003 013 200        DELAY
003 014 003        0
003 015 303        JMP     /UNCONDITIONAL JUMP TO "LOOP"
003 016 007        LOOP
003 017 003        0
/
/SUBROUTINE: DELAY
/DESCRIPTION: THIS SUBROUTINE GENERATES
/A 0.1 SECOND DELAY FOR A MICROCOMPUTER
/OPERATING WITH A 750 KHZ CLOCK
/
          *003 200
003 200 365  DELAY, PUSHPSW /SAVE MICROCOMPUTER STATUS
003 201 325        PUSHD
003 202 021        LXID    /LOAD REGISTER PAIR D WITH
003 203 250        250     /TIMING BYTES FOR
003 204 015        015     /0.1 SECOND DELAY
003 205 033  LOOP1, DCXD
003 206 173        MOVAE
003 207 262        ORAD    /TIMING BYTE ZERO?
003 210 302        JNZ     /NO, KEEP DECREASING
003 211 205        LOOP1
003 212 003        0
003 213 321        POPD    /YES, RESTORE MICROCOMPUTER STATUS
003 214 361        POPPSW
003 215 311        RET
```

Fig. 3-10. Program for Experiment 3-1.

(b) To illustrate the use of the 8255 in mode 0 operation for data output.

Step 1

Connect the circuit shown in the schematic diagram in Fig. 3-11. Inputs A0, A1, and A7 are available on the memory address bus.

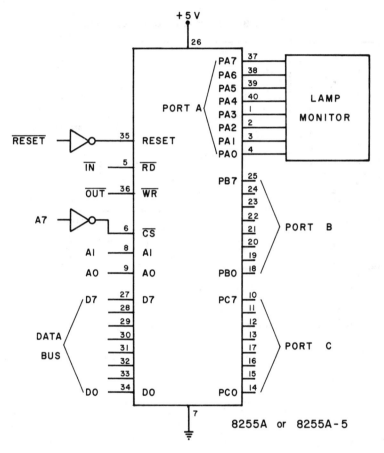

Fig. 3-11. Use of 8255 IC.

Since two identical sets of device codes appear on address lines A0 through A7 and A8 through A15 during an OUT or IN instruction, bits A7 and A15 are identical in this case.

Make certain that the proper connections are made to the RESET input at pin 35 on the 8255 chip. The author once had a faulty

RESET connection and spent two hours trying to track down the problem, which he thought was elsewhere in the circuit.

Step 2

The truth table for the operation of the 8255 programmable peripheral interface chip is shown in Table 3-2.

Table 3-2. Basic Operation of 8255 IC

A₁	A₀	$\overline{RD}$	$\overline{WR}$	$\overline{CS}$	Input Operation (Read)
0	0	0	1	0	Port A → Data Bus
0	1	0	1	0	Port B → Data Bus
1	0	0	1	0	Port C → Data Bus
					Output Operation (Write)
0	0	1	0	0	Data Bus → Port A
0	1	1	0	0	Data Bus → Port B
1	0	1	0	0	Data Bus → Port C
1	1	1	0	0	Data Bus → Control
					Disable Function
X	X	X	X	1	Data Bus → 3-State
1	1	0	1	0	Illegal Condition

Schematic Diagram of Circuit (Fig. 3-11)

Study the truth table in Table 3-3 for the four control inputs to the 8255 chip. Assume that input $\overline{CS}$ is at logic 0, i.e., A7 is at logic 1.

Keep in mind that the address bus has the following significance when used to address our 8255 chip:

Bit:	A7	A6	A5	A4	A3	A2	A1	A0
Input:	$\overline{CS}$	X	X	X	X	X	A1	A0

An X indicates that the logic state of the address bit is unimportant.

What device address value is needed if you wish to write a control byte into the control register?

To write into the control register, A7 must be logic 1, A1 must be at logic 1, and A0 must be at logic 1, according to the truth table. Therefore the device code is:

Table 3-3. Control Inputs to 8255 IC

OUT	IN	A1	A0	Action
0	1	0	0	Data Bus → Port A
0	1	0	1	Data Bus → Port B
0	1	1	0	Data Bus → Port C
0	1	1	1	Data Bus → Control Register
1	0	0	0	Port A → Data Bus
1	0	0	1	Port B → Data Bus
1	0	1	0	Port C → Data Bus
1	0	1	1	Not Allowed
1	1	0	0	Data Bus → 3-State
1	1	0	1	Data Bus → 3-State
1	1	1	0	Data Bus → 3-State
1	1	1	1	Data Bus → 3-State
0	0	X	X	Not Allowed

$$1XXXXX11$$

If we set X equal to logic 0, then the device address is simply 10000011, or 203. This is the technique that we use to address the 8255 chip.

Step 3

The mode 0 configuration that you will first test is for the mode 0 control word which is given by Intel Corporation as in Fig. 3-12. This is the value of the 8-bit control word, MODE, that must appear

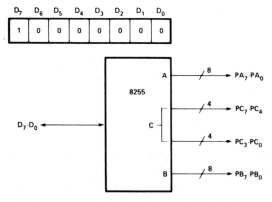

Fig. 3-12. Mode 0 control word and schematic diagram.

at LO memory address 004 in the program. The schematic diagram indicates that you will output data to port A on the 8255 chip. The device address for port A is simply 200, according to the truth table provided in Step 2. This device code, DATA, must appear at LO memory address 010 in the program.

Step 4

Load the program into memory. Make certain that the mode control word and the PPI I/O device code are correct.

Step 5

Execute the program. What do you observe on the pair of lamp monitor Outboards™* connected to port A?

We observed that the lamp monitors incremented at a rate of approximately 10 Hz.

Step 6

Relocate the pair of lamp monitor Outboards to port B. Change the PPI I/O device address at LO memory address 010 to 201. Execute the program. What do you observe?

We observed that the lamp monitors again incremented at a rate of approximately 10 Hz.

Step 7

Relocate the pair of lamp monitor Outboards to port C. Change the device address at LO memory address 010 to 202. Execute the program. What do you observe now?

We again observed that the lamp monitors at port C incremented at a rate of approximately 10 Hz.

---

* OUTBOARD is a registered trademark of E & L Instruments, Inc.

To summarize, the program values that you have used so far are the following:

Control word : 200   Establishes mode 0 PPI operation and sets up ports A through C as output ports.

Port A (output): 200
Port B (output): 201
Port C (output): 202   I/O device codes for ports A through C, respectively.

Step 8

With the pair of lamp monitor Outboards still located at port C, change the mode control word, MODE, at memory address 004 to that shown in Fig. 3-13. Execute the program. What do you observe on the pair of lamp monitor Outboards? Explain your observations.

We observed that only the LEDs connected to the port C lower pins (PC0–PC3) were incrementing. This is because the mode control word 210 configures port C lower for output but port C upper for input. Hence, even though 8 bits are output to port C, only the lower four bits are displayed.

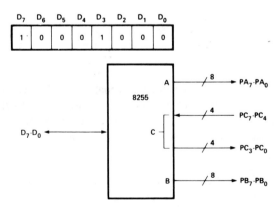

Fig. 3-13. Second mode control word.

Step 9

With the pair of lamp monitor Outboards still located at port C, now change "MODE" at memory address 004 to that shown in Fig. 3-14. Execute the program. What do you observe on the pair of lamp monitor Outboards? Explain your observations.

We found that this time the LEDs connected to port C upper were slowly incrementing while those connected to port C lower were not lit. This is because the mode control word 201 configures port C upper for output but port C lower for input. Only the top four bits of the 8-bit byte, which is sent to port C, are thus displayed.

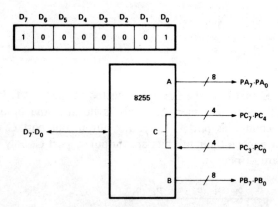

Fig. 3-14. Third mode control word.

Step 10

With the pair of lamp monitor Outboards still located at port C, change the control word at LO memory address 004 to the control word shown in Fig. 3-15. Execute the revised program and explain what you observe on the pair of lamp monitor Outboards.

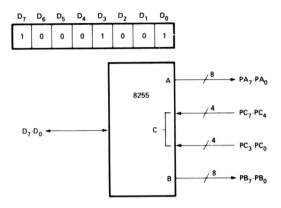

Fig. 3-15. Fourth mode control word.

This time no LEDs were lit during program execution since mode control word 211 configures both port C upper and lower for input. Thus none of the bits of the 8-bit byte, which is sent to port C from the accumulator, are displayed.

NOTE: Remove the lamp monitor Outboards that are connected to port C. Do not make any other changes to your hardware if you plan to go on to the next experiment.

Questions

1. What device code and input/output command (i.e., either IN or OUT) are required if you wish *to read the data* appearing *at port A?* Set all Xs to logic 0.

2. What device code and input/output command are required if you wish *to output data to port B?* Set all Xs to logic 0.

3. What device code and input/output command are required if you wish *to output data to port C?* Set all Xs to logic 0.

4. How many device codes could be used for the input and output operations to the 8255 chip? You can assume that each X can be either logic 0 or logic 1.

5. Suggest at least one way to decrease the number of possible device codes used, as calculated in Question No. 4 above. If necessary, draw a schematic diagram of your circuit.

6. What device code and control signals, if any, allow you to read the status of the 8-bit control register?

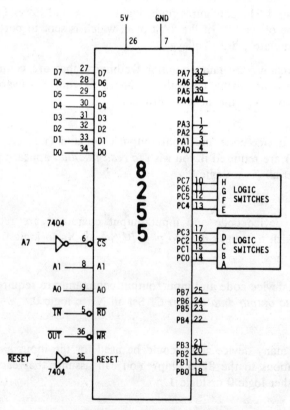

Fig. 3-16. Circuit for Experiment 3-2.

EXPERIMENT 3-2
MODE 0 DATA INPUT OPERATION

Purpose

The purpose of this experiment is to illustrate the *mode 0 operation* of the 8255 for *input of data into the accumulator* via the 8255 chip from a pair of logic switch Outboards.

Schematic Diagram of Circuit (Fig. 3-16)

NOTE: This circuit is the same as that which was connected in Experiment 3-1 except for the use of logic switches in place of lamp monitors at the port A through C lines.

Program (Fig. 3-17)

```
            /
            /PPI MODE 0 INPUT PROGRAM
            /
            DB MODE 233
            DB DATA 202
            DB CNTRL 203
            *003 000
003 000 076          MVIA     /LOAD A WITH
003 001 233          MODE     /MODE 0 CONTROL BYTE
003 002 323          OUT      /OUTPUT CONTENTS OF A TO
003 003 203          CNTRL    /CONTROL REGISTER
003 004 333   LOOP,  IN       /INPUT DATA FROM
003 005 202          DATA     /PPI INPUT PORT
003 006 323          OUT      /OUTPUT IT TO PORT 2
003 007 002          002
003 010 303          JMP      /JUMP TO LOOP AT
003 011 004          LOOP
003 012 003          0
```

Fig. 3-17. Program for Experiment 3-2.

Step 1

Wire the circuit shown in the schematic diagram of Fig. 3-16 if it is not already connected from the previous experiment. The mode 0 configuration that you will first test is the mode 0 control word, which is shown in Fig. 3-18. This is the value of the 8-bit control word that you should enter at LO memory address 001 in the program.

The schematic diagram of Fig. 3-18 indicates that you will input data through port C on the 8255 chip. The device for port C is 202, according to the truth table provided in Experiment 3-1. This device code must appear at LO memory address 005 in the program.

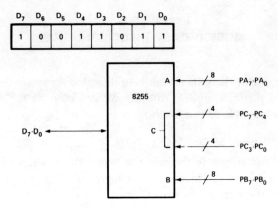

Fig. 3-18. Mode 0 control and schematic diagram.

Step 2

Load the program into read/write memory. Make certain that the mode control word and the PPI input/output device code are correct.

Step 3

Execute the program. While the microcomputer is running, alter the logic switch settings and observe at output port 002 the bytes which are being input. What happens?

We observed that the 8-bit byte, which is set on the logic switches, is continuously displayed at output port 002. Any alteration to the logic switches produced an immediate corresponding change at output port 002.

Step 4

Relocate the pair of logic switch Outboard to port B. Change the device address at LO memory address 005 to 201. Execute the program. What happens now?

We again observed that the byte displayed at output port 2 was the same as that set up at port B of the PPI by the logic switches.

Step 5

Finally, relocate the pair of logic switch Outboards to port A. Change the device code at LO memory address 005 to 200. Execute the program. Do you still observe the bytes which are input from the logic switches at port A being displayed at output port 002 when the program is run? You should.

EXPERIMENT 3-3
COMBINED MODE 0 INPUT AND OUTPUT OPERATION

Purpose

The purpose of this experiment is to illustrate the mode 0 operation of the 8255 chip for combined input and output using port C

Schematic Diagram of Circuit (Fig. 3-19)

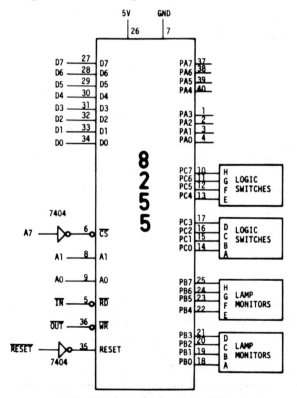

Fig. 3-19. Circuit for Experiment 3-3.

Program (Fig. 3-20)

```
                /
                /PPI MODE 0 COMBINED INPUT AND OUTPUT PROGRAM
                /
                DB MODE 232
                DB CNTRL 203
                DB DATA1 202
                DB DATA2 201
                *003 000
003 000 076          MVIA     /LOAD A WITH
003 001 232          MODE     /MODE 0 CONTROL WORD
003 002 323          OUT      /OUTPUT CONTENTS OF A TO
003 003 203          CNTRL    /CONTROL REGISTER
003 004 333   LOOP,  IN       /LOAD A WITH THE CONTENTS
003 005 202          DATA1    /OF THE PPI INPUT PORT
003 006 000          NOP
003 007 000          NOP
003 010 323          OUT      /OUTPUT CONTENTS OF A TO
003 011 201          DATA2    /PPI OUTPUT PORT
003 012 303          JMP      /JUMP TO "LOOP"
003 013 004          LOOP
003 014 003          0
```

Fig. 3-20. Program for Experiment 3-3.

for input and port B for output. Port A will also be assigned for output. This experiment is a synthesis of the procedures illustrated individually in Experiments 3-1 and 3-2 for output and input of data, respectively. If you feel that you have grasped the procedures required for the mode 0 input/output operation of the PPI, you might like to write and test a program to input data from the logic switches at port C, and output this data to the lamp monitors at port B (or port A). The author has written a program if you would prefer not to attempt a program at this stage. The decision on this experiment is yours—have fun!

Step 1

The mode 0 configuration that you will test first is defined by the mode control word in Fig. 3-21. This is the value of the 8-bit control word, MODE, that appears at LO memory address 001 in the program of Fig. 3-20. The schematic diagram of Fig. 3-21 indicates that you will input data through port C, which has device code 202, and output data back through port B, which has device code 201. These two device addresses should appear, respectively, at LO memory addresses 005 and 011.

76

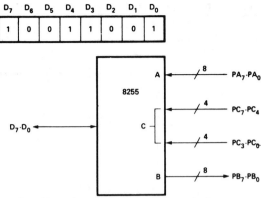

Fig. 3-21. Mode control word and schematic diagram.

Step 2

Load the program into read/write memory. Make certain that the control word and the two device addresses are correct.

Step 3

Execute the program. While the microcomputer is running, alter the logic switch settings and observe the output at port B. What happens?

We observed that the data byte which was set by the logic switches at port C was continuously displayed at port B and immediately updated whenever the switches were altered.

Step 4

Relocate the pair of lamp monitors to port A. Change the device address at LO memory address 011 to 200, which is the port A device address; and the mode control word at LO memory address 001 to 213, which configures the PPI as shown in Fig. 3-22.

Execute the program once more and again alter the logic switch settings. What happens now?

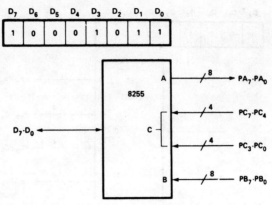

Fig. 3-22. Second mode control word and schematic diagram.

This time the data byte which was set by the logic switches at port C was continuously displayed at port A and again immediately updated whenever the logic switches were altered.

Step 5

Add the following instructions to your program in place of the two no-operation (NOP) instructions at 003 006 and 003 007:

003 006	346	ANI
003 007	272	272

Now run your program and set each switch position in turn from logic zero to logic one. What happens at Port A?

We observed that the lamps corresponding to bits PC6, PC2, and PC0 would not go on. Why?

The bits in the immediate AND byte for these positions are zero. Anything ANDed with 0 yields a result of 0.

Step 6

Now replace the instruction at memory location 003 006 with the following instruction:

Execute your program and explain what you observe at port A when the logic switches are set, in turn, from logic 0 to logic 1.

We observed that a LED at port A would light wherever the logic state of a bit at port C was opposite to the corresponding bit in the immediate byte, 272, at location 003 007. This is because the exclusive-OR logic function is a difference detector and gives a logic 1 result when the two bits being exclusive-ORed are different.

Steps 7, 8, . . . , etc.

We invite you to try for yourself the following instructions, in turn, at location 003 006.

366	ORI
306	ADI
326	SUI

4

PPI Bit-Set/Reset Operation

4-1. INTRODUCTION

The bit-set/reset feature of the 8255 was mentioned briefly in Section 2-1(D) of Chapter 2. We saw that it is essentially a feature of port C which allows the user to individually set or reset any of its bits. To use this property of port C a bit-set/reset control word must be sent to the PPI control register. The format of this control word was presented in Chapter 2 and is reproduced again in Fig. 4-1.

Note that it is the most significant bit (D7) of the control word that determines whether the control byte will be interpreted by the 8255 as a *mode* control word (D7 = 1) or a *bit-set/reset* control word (D7 = 0). Other important features of this control word are:

- Bits D3, D2, and D1 of the bit-set/reset control word represent a 3-bit code, the binary value of which defines the port C bit (PC0–PC7) which is to be set or reset.
- The logic state of bit D0 specifies whether the selected port C bit is to be set (D0 = 1) or reset (D0 = 0). This means that each bit-set/reset control word can be used to set or reset only one of the port C bits at a time. If, for example, port C bit PC0 (D3 D2 D1 = 000) had been set (D0 = 1) by outputting a bit-set/reset control word to the PPI control word register, a second bit-set/reset control word would be needed to reset PC0.
- Bits D6, D5, and D4 are unused and are usually set to 0. However, as you will see in Experiment 4-1, they are "don't care" bits and any logic values can be used for these bits.

Having looked at the control word that is output to the PPI control register to independently set or reset any one of the port C bits, it is not unreasonable to ask why such a feature is incorporated in the 8255. The main reason is concerned with the mode 1 and 2 operations of the PPI which are described in the next three chapters. Let us just say for the moment that operating modes 1 and 2 are used for unidirectional and bidirectional handshaking I/O, respectively, with interrupt capability. The port C bits are employed as handshaking control bits for port A and port B. These control bits are

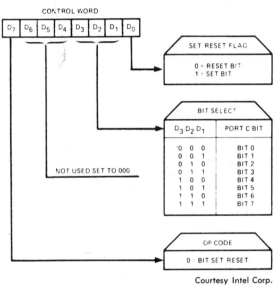

Courtesy Intel Corp.

Fig. 4-1. The format of the bit-set/reset control word.

configured so that the port A or port B interrupt flags will be set once an external peripheral has acknowledged an I/O transfer. Associated with each interrupt flag is an *interrupt enable flip-flop* which can be set or reset using the bit-set/reset feature of port C. The details of how and why this is done will be explained in Chapters 6 and 7.

A second simpler, but equally important, use for the port C bit-set/reset facility is to generate logic levels and pulses of varying duration that can be used as gating pulses and hardware reset pulses for counters, flip-flops, etc. In general the port C bits, when used with the bit-set/reset control word, can be used for the gating, strobing, and reset functions that are normally associated with device select or address select pulses.* The major advantage to using the PPI port C bits for these functions is that no additional hardware is needed. This is certainly the case for the generation of short duration (approximately 8 µs) pulses where the software requirements, as shown in Fig. 4-2, are simple. The software is, however, somewhat more complex than that required to generate device select or address select pulses. Note that a DCR A instruction has been used in the program flowchart shown in Fig. 4-2. This instruction changes the control word from its set to reset function.

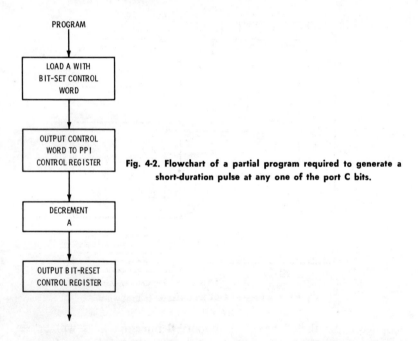

Fig. 4-2. Flowchart of a partial program required to generate a short-duration pulse at any one of the port C bits.

The pulse duration in the above case would be approximately 7.5 µs for a microcomputer operating at a 2-MHz clock frequency. This is the time required to execute the decrement and output instructions. Gating pulses of controlled duration can be generated by inserting known time delays following the first output instruction. On occasions, however, it may be more effective to set and reset an external flip-flop using two bits of port C. The use of port C bits for gating and hardware reset is illustrated in Experiment 4-2.

---

*See *Introductory Experiments in Digital Electronics and 8080A Microcomputer Programming and Interfacing,* Book 2, Unit 17.

4-2. PROCEDURE FOR SETTING AND RESETTING PORT C BITS

To illustrate the use of the bit-set/reset control byte, let us write a program to set and reset port C bit PC5. From Fig. 4-1 the bit-set/reset control bytes needed to set and reset bit PC5 are constructed as follows:

D7:	Function code = 0 for bit-set/reset operation
D6,D5,D4:	Unused
D3,D2,D1:	Port C bit select = 101_2 for PC5
D0:	Set/reset select flag = 1 for bit set
	= 0 for bit reset

Hence the PC5 bit-set/reset control word format is:

$$0\ 0\ 0\ 0\ 1\ 0\ 1\ 1/0$$
$$= 013_8 \text{ for bit set}$$
$$= 012_8 \text{ for bit reset}$$

The flow diagram for this example is the same as that shown in Fig. 4-2. A program listing that is the equivalent of this flowchart is given in Program 4-1. The only addition is the PPI initialization statements which must be executed in a program before any attempt is made to use the PPI.

Program 4-1 (Fig 4-3)

In this program we have not specified a value for the mode control byte. By now you will understand that its value depends on the way in which the PPI is to be configured. The only thing that can be said for the moment is that since bit PC5 is used for output, bit D3 (port C upper I/O select) of the mode control word will need to be set at logic 0 (*cf* Fig. 2-2A). The control register device code has also been left unspecified since this is a function of the hardware address decoding to the PPI.

Three further points are of interest in relation to this program example of bit-set/reset operation:

1. At memory location 003 010, a single-byte DCR A instruction was used to change the bit-set control byte in the accumulator to a bit-reset control byte. This is possible since the bit-*reset* control byte is one less than the bit-*set* control byte. The tech-

```
                        /
                        /A PROGRAM TO SET & RESET PORT C BIT PC5
                        /
                        DB CNTRL 203
                        *003 000
003 000 076             MVI A        /LOAD A WITH
003 001                 MODE         /MODE CONTROL BYTE
003 002 323             OUT          /OUTPUT IT
003 003 203             CNTRL        /CONTROL REGISTER DEVICE CODE
003 004 076     LOOP,   MVI A        /LOAD A WITH PC5 BIT-SET
003 005 013             013          /CONTROL BYTE
003 006 323             OUT          /OUTPUT IT
003 007 203             CNTRL        /CONTROL REGISTER DEVICE CODE
003 010 075             DCR A        /DECREMENT A TO GENERATE A BIT
                                     /RESET CONTROL BYTE
003 011 323             OUT          /OUTPUT PC5 BIT RESET
003 012 203             CNTRL        /CONTROL BYTE TO CONTROL REGISTER
003 013 303             JMP          /LOOP TO GENERATE ANOTHER PULSE
003 014 004             LOOP
003 015 003             0
```

Fig. 4-3. Program 4-1.

nique of using this one-byte instruction instead of the two-byte
instruction:

MVI A

BITRST

is recommended since it conserves memory space which, on
occasions, may be critical, and also since it is slightly faster
(five clock cycles compared with seven for the MVI A,
which, on occasions, may be critical, and also since it is slightly
faster (five clock cycles compared with seven for the MVI A,
BITRST instruction). The decrement instruction could not be
used, of course, if instructions which altered the accumulator
contents were to follow the bit-set output instruction and pre-
cede the bit-reset output instruction.

2. The pulses generated by Program 4-1 are *active high,* i.e., the
   PC5 logic state is normally low and goes high momentarily. A
   complementary, or inverted, active low pulse can be generated
   with essentially the same software by outputting a bit-reset
   control byte first, *incrementing* the accumulator, and then outputting the resulting bit-set control byte. In doing this it is
   assumed that PC5 was initially at logic one. Now Experiment
   4-1 illustrates how loading the control register of the PPI with
   a mode control byte *resets all bits of port C to logic 0.* Hence
   in this program the initial state of PC5 is logic 0 and so PC5
   would need to be initialized to logic 1 using a bit-set control

byte prior to entering the loop that commences at location 003 004. This is illustrated in Program 4-2. The simple software changes illustrated in Program 4-2 avoid the need for an inverter and again serve to illustrate the advantage of programmed logic (the PPI and microcomputer in this case) in replacing hardware with software.

3. To generate a longer-duration gating signal using Program 4-1, a call to a time-delay subroutine would need to be inserted between the two output commands (*cf* Program 4-2). This routine would then delay the resetting of PC5 for as long as is required. After returning from the delay routine the accumulator would need to be loaded with the bit-reset control word for output to the PPI control register. Whether a DCR A or MVI A instruction is used to do this depends on whether the

Program 4-2 (Fig. 4-4)

```
            /
            /THIS PROGRAM GENERATES, AT PORT C BIT PC5, AN
            /ACTIVE LOW PULSE WHOSE DURATION IS CONTROLLED
            /BY A CALL TO SUBROUTINE DELAY
            /
            DB MODE 200      /THIS IS AN ARBITARY FIGURE
            DB CNTRL 203     /THIS IS ALSO AN ARBITARY FIGURE
            DW DELAY1 003 200 /STARTING ADDRESSES OF
            DW DELAY2 003 220 /DELAY SUBROUTINES
            *003 000
003 000 076 START,  MVIA     /INITIALIZE PPI
003 001 200         MODE
003 002 323         OUT
003 003 203         CNTRL
003 004 076         MVIA     /LOAD A WITH A CONTROL BYTE
003 005 013         013      /TO SET PC5 TO LOGIC ONE
003 006 323         OUT
003 007 203         CNTRL
003 010 076 LOOP,   MVIA     /LOAD A WITH A CONTROL BYTE
003 011 012         012      /TO RESET PC5 TO LOGIC ZERO
003 012 323         OUT
003 013 203         CNTRL
003 014 315         CALL     /CALL DELAY1 SUBROUTINE TO GENERATE
003 015 200         DELAY1   /THE REQUIRED PULSE WIDTH
003 016 003         0
003 017 074         INRA     /INCREMENT A TO FORM THE PC5 BIT
                             /SET CONTROL BYTE
003 020 323         OUT
003 021 203         CNTRL
003 022 315         CALL     /CALL DELAY2 SUBROUTINE TO GENERATE
003 023 220         DELAY2   /THE PERIOD BETWEEN PULSES
003 024 003         0
003 025 303         JMP
003 026 010         LOOP
003 027 003         0
```

Fig. 4-4. Program 4-2.

time-delay routine destroys the accumulator contents. Clearly the MVI A instruction would need to be used if the accumulator contents are destroyed. However, it is common practice in writing subroutines to save the status of any registers (using PUSH instructions) which are used by the subroutine and to restore their original status (using POP instructions) before returning from the subroutine. Hence, it will generally be safe to use a DCRA instruction. Check the subroutine first through before deciding.

4-3. EXAMPLE: A VALVE CONTROLLER

(A) The Physical Process and Its Control Interface

In this section we have a practical example of the way in which the port C bit-set/reset feature of the PPI can be used to control and sequence the operation of a microcomputer interface. Our example concerns the establishment of vacuum conditions in a chemical reactor. The absolute pressure in the reactor is to be reduced to approximately 5×10^{-3} mm of mercury (i.e., 5×10^{-3} torr), a value which can be conveniently established using a vacuum backing pump. The pressure in the reactor vessel is measured using a thermistor pressure gauge which is placed in the vacuum line to the vessel.

Fig. 4-5 shows a schematic diagram of the vacuum line and the controller interface to the PPI. A solenoid valve is placed between the backing pump and the reactor so that the reactor can be isolated from the backing pump once vacuum conditions have been established. The sequence of events that are controlled by the microcomputer is as follows:

- Turn on the vacuum backing pump.
- Open the solenoid pressure valve.
- Monitor the pressure.
- Close the solenoid valve when the pressure reaches the required set point value (5×10^{-3} torr in this case).

Both the pump and the solenoid valve are 110 Vac operated and can therefore be switched on and off by switching the voltage on and off using solid-state relays. These devices are cheap (a few dollors) and can switch up to 10 amperes at 110 volts with a dc switching voltage between 3 and 32 V across their dc inputs. The normal condition of the pressure valve is closed. When 110 Vac is applied, a solenoid coil is energized and a metal slug, which is

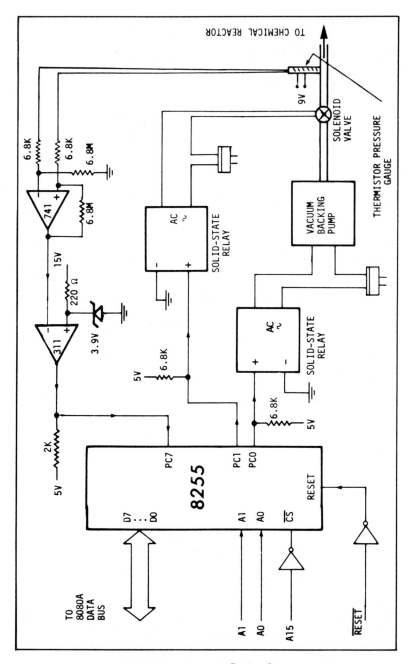

Fig. 4-5. A vacuum controller interface.

attached to a spring-loaded valve, is raised to open the valve. The valve stays open as long as the voltage is applied to the solenoid. Hence, in the interface which is depicted in Fig. 4-5, bits PC0 and PC1 of port C are used to switch two solid-state relays that are connected to the backing pump and the solenoid valve, respectively.

An interesting feature of port B and C of the PPI that is used here is that *any set of eight lines can provide approximately 2-mA drive current each when the output voltage is 1.5 V.* This drive current, even when the outputs are greater than 3 V (using the pull-up resistor) is sufficient to drive the dc inputs of the solid-state relays and to switch them on when the PC0 and PC1 outputs are at a logic high. This avoids the need for buffers between the outputs of the PPI and the solid-state relays.

The thermistor pressure gauge, like most transducers, has an output voltage that is not suitable for direct connection to a PPI (PC7 in this case). At atmospheric pressure its output voltage is approximately 120 mV, while at an absolute pressure of approximately 5×10^{-3} torr, its output voltage is approximately 4 mV. These potentials are said to be "floating" as they are not referenced to a ground (0 V). The operational amplifiers in Fig. 4-5 are used to produce an input signal at PC7 of the PPI which is normally at 0 V (logic 0) and rises to +5 V (logic 1) when the system pressure reaches 5×10^{-3} torr.

(B) The PPI and the Controlling Program

The PPI has been connected to an 8080A-based microcomputer, in this example, for memory-mapped I/O. Following the discussion in Section 2-1, it can be seen that the *device addresses* in this case are:

PORT C : 200 002
CONTROL REGISTER : 200 003

The labels PORT C and CNTRL have been defined with these values, in the controller program which is listed in Fig. 4-6.

Program 4-3 (Fig. 4-6)

We must now construct the *mode control byte,* MODE, which will configure port C upper for input to accept the pressure flag; and configure port C lower for output so that the two solid-state relays can be switched on and off. Although not used, ports A and B will be configured for mode 0 input. The required mode control byte can be constructed from Fig. 2-2A and is:

```
                    /
                    /VACUUM VALVE CONTROLLER PROGRAM
                    /
                    DB MODE 232
                    DW PORTC 200 002
                    DW CNTRL 200 003
                    DW DELAY 003 200
                    *003 000
003 000 061    START,  LXISP   /SET STACK POINTER
003 001 000            000
003 002 004            004
003 003 041            LXIH    /SET UP PPI DEVICE ADDRESS
003 004 003            CNTRL   /FOR THE CONTROL REGISTER
003 005 200            0
003 006 021            LXID    /LOAD THE D REGISTER PAIR WITH
003 007 003            003     /PCI BITSET CONTROL BYTE IN D
003 010 001            001     /PCO BITSET CONTROL BYTE IN E
003 011 076            MVIA    /LOAD ACCUMULATOR WITH MODE
003 012 232            MODE    /CONTROL BYTE
003 013 167            MOVMA   /OUTPUT IT TO CONTROL REGISTER
003 014 163            MOVME   /SWITCH ON BACKING PUMP
003 015 162            MOVMD   /OPEN SOLENOID VALVE
003 016 053            DCXH    /SET UP PORT C ADDRESS IN H,L
003 017 176    LOOP,   MOVAM   /INPUT PRESSURE FLAG
003 020 346            ANI     /MASK PC7
003 021 200            200
003 022 312            JZ      /IS VACUUM ESTABLISHED
003 023 017            LOOP    /NO, LOOK AGAIN
003 024 003            0
003 025 315            CALL    /YES, WAIT FOR ONE SECOND
003 026 200            DELAY
003 027 003            0
003 030 176            MOVAM   /AND LOOK AGAIN
003 031 346            ANI     /MASK PC7
003 032 200            200
003 033 312            JZ      /IS VACUUM STILL ESTABLISHED
003 034 017            LOOP    /NO, LOOK AGAIN
003 035 003            0
003 036 043            INXH    /YES,SET ADDRESS OF CONTROL REGISTER
003 037 172            MOVAD   /CONSTRUCT PCI BIT-RESET CONTROL BYTE
003 040 075            DCRA
003 041 167            MOVMA   /AND USE IT TO CLOSE VALVE
                    /         .
                    /         .
                    /         .
                    /         .
                    /         .
```

Fig. 4-6. Program 4-3.

MODE : 232

Since port C bits PC0 and PC1 must be set and reset to control the backing pump and solenoid valve respectively, *bit-set/reset control bytes* will be required. We will define bit-set control bytes for PC0 (PC0SET) and PC1 (PC1SET) and decrement their respective values in the program to obtain bit-reset control bytes. From Fig. 2-2B the required values are:

PC0SET : 001

PC1SET : 003

Remembering now that the PPI is connected to the microcomputer for memory-mapped I/O, a program which will establish vacuum conditions in the reactor following the sequence of events described above, is listed as Program 4-3 (Fig. 4-6). After initializing the PPI with port C upper configured for input and port C lower configured for output, the program then switches on the backing pump and opens the solenoid valve by setting PC0 and PC1 to logic 1 respectively. The pressure flag is then monitored by inputting the contents of port C and masking out all bits except PC7. When PC7 is at logic 1 a 1-second delay is generated and the flag is checked again as described above. Because the system pressure changes very slowly as it approaches 5×10^{-3} torr the initial detection of PC7 at logic 1 may represent only a transient excursion of the system pressure down to 5×10^{-3} torr. The delay ensures that a steady value of the required pressure has been established. When this is the case the solenoid valve is closed by resetting port C bit PC0 to logic 0.

The feature of the programming in this example is the use of the MOV M,r memory reference instruction to output bit-set and bit-reset control bytes to the PPI, which is connected as a memory-mapped I/O port. In this case register pair H has been used to initially store the device address of the PPI's control register. The address of port C is then obtained by decrementing the H register pair with a DCX H instruction. At the end of the program the H register pair is incremented (INX H) to again establish the device address of the control register, so that a PC1 bit-reset control byte can be sent to the control register of the PPI to switch off the solenoid valve. Care must be exercised in establishing device addresses for the PPI through this incrementation and decrementation technique, since the risk always exists that you may lose track of "where you are up to," or that the H register pair contents may be altered in a subroutine call. Note also that registers D and E are used to store the PC1 and PC0 bit-set control bytes respectively. These bytes are then output directly to the control register of the PPI with MOV M,D and MOV M,E instructions.

In conclusion, the example has illustrated the use of the port C bit-set/reset feature for control and sequencing the operation of a vacuum line. Hardware is reduced to a minimum through the ability to set, and later to reset, the bits of port C. The high-current drive of each bit of port C for logic 1 outputs eliminates the need for buffer drivers where devices are being driven to a logic 1. (Note that the fan-out of each of the bits of port C for a logic 0 is only one standard TTL load). The software is straightforward and involves the initialization of the PPI, the sending of bit-set and bit-reset control bytes to the PPI's control register, and the polling of port C for the logic state of PC7

4-4. SUMMARY OF EXPERIMENTS 4-1 AND 4-2

Experiment	Description
4-1	This experiment illustrates how the *bit-set/reset control word* can be used to set and reset individual bits of port C; and how the *code control word* resets all the bits of port C.
4-2	In this experiment you will: (a) Use the bit-set/reset operation of the PPI to gate pulses into a counter. (b) Input the data from the counter using mode 0 simple I/O. (c) Reset the counter using the PPI set/reset feature of port C.

EXPERIMENT 4-1
SETTING AND RESETTING OF PORT C

Purpose

The aims of this experiment are the following:
(a) To set and reset the individual bits of port C using the bit-set/reset format of the control word; and
(b) To show that the bits of port C are reset by:
    (i) A logic high to the PPI's reset pin; and
    (ii) Outputting a mode control byte to the control register.

Step 1

Wire the circuit shown in the schematic diagram of Fig. 4-7 and load the program into the microcomputer's read/write memory.

Step 2

Insert a halt instruction (HLT = 166) for the first NOP instruction at address 003 011. Start the program. Have any of the lamps at port C been turned on?

Schematic Diagram of Circuit (Fig. 4-7)

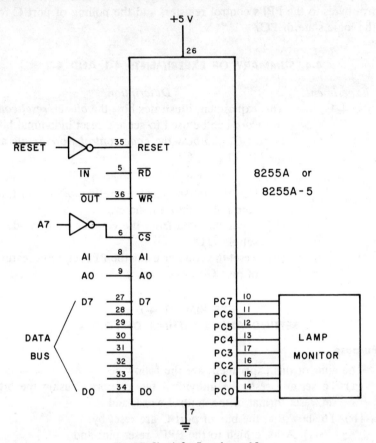

Fig. 4-7. Circuit for Experiment 4-1.

Yes, we observed that bit PC0 was on (logic 1). Is this consistent with the chart provided in Fig. 4-1?

Yes, a bit-set/reset control byte of 001 will set bit PC0.

Step 3

Can you determine the bit-set/reset control bytes that are needed to set bits PC3, PC5, and PC6 to logic 1, one at a time? (See Fig. 4-1.)

Program (Fig. 4-8)

```
            /
            /THIS PROGRAM ILLUSTRATES THE SETTING &
            /RESETTING OF BITS PC0 TO PC7 OF PORT C
            /
            DB CNTRL 203
            *003 000
003 000 016       MVIC    /LOAD REGISTER C WITH
003 001 200       200     /MODE CONTROL BYTE
003 002 171       MOVAC   /COPY MODE CONTROL BYTE TO A
003 003 323       OUT     /OUTPUT IT TO PPI CONTROL
003 004 203       CNTRL   /REGISTER
003 005 076       MVIA    /LOAD ACCUMULATOR WITH THE
003 006 001       001     /BIT-SET CONTROL WORD
003 007 323       OUT     /OUTPUT IT TO PPI CONTROL
003 010 203       CNTRL   /REGISTER
003 011 000       NOP
003 012 000       NOP
003 013 000       NOP
003 014 075       DCRA    /DECREMENT A
003 015 323       OUT     /OUTPUT BIT-RESET CONTROL BYTE
003 016 203       CNTRL   /TO CONTROL REGISTER
003 017 166       HLT
```

Fig. 4-8. Program for Experiment 4-1.

Mode Control Byte
PC3
PC4
PC5

We used control bytes of 007, 013, and 015, respectively. Insert these control bytes, one at a time, for the bit-set control byte at address 003 006 and run the program. Do the appropriate bits become logic 1?

Yes, they do, but only one at a time. Bits PC3, PC5, and PC6 were not set simultaneously to logic 1. How would you set up a program to leave all 3 bits set at a logic 1 after the program was executed?

We suggest the sequence shown in Fig. 4-9. This sequence will leave all the bits "on" after the program has been run.

```
MVI A     /SET PC3
007
OUT
203
MVI A     /SET PC5
013
OUT
203
MVI A     /SET PC6
015
OUT
203
HLT
```

Fig. 4-9. Sequence to leave PC3, PC5, and PC6 at logic 1.

Step 4

Remove the halt instruction at address 003 011 by replacing it and the two following NOP instructions with a call to the DELAY subroutine:

```
003 011    315    CALL
003 012    200    DELAY
003 013    003     φ
```

Enter the delay subroutine, DELAY, which is listed in Fig. 3-10 if it is not already entered in your microcomputer.

Step 5

Be sure to reinsert the PC0 bit-set control byte of 001 at address 003 006. Start the microcomputer and observe any changes in the lamp monitors. What happens?

The lamp monitoring bit PC0 comes on (logic 1) and then goes off. The on period is about 0.1 second. Why is this activity observed?

A bit-set control byte is output to the PPI and the time-delay subroutine is then executed. After the time delay is finished, the program outputs a bit-reset control byte to the PPI. The on time can be varied by changing the timing bytes in the DELAY subroutine.

Step 6

To demonstrate the software control of the on time, change the timing bytes in the DELAY subroutines to 377 377. Again try the program. What do you see?

The on time should be approximately 2 seconds.

Step 7

In this step you will examine the effect of an external reset on the logic state of the port C outputs. To see the effect, replace the CALL instruction (315) at address 003 011 with a halt instruction (HLT). Load the bit-set control byte 001 into location 003 006. This will set bit PC0 to a logic 1. Start the program. What happens? Reset your computer with its reset push button or switch. What happens now? Why?

When the program was run, we saw the lamp monitor for bit PC0 come on (logic 1). When the computer was reset it went off. This property of the PPI's reset function applies to all of the port C bits. You may wish to confirm this by repeating this step with different bit-set control bytes at location 003 006.

Step 8

Another method of resetting all of the bits of port C to logic 0 is by outputting a mode control byte to the control register of the PPI. This, of course, is not the main function of the mode control byte but is an interesting and useful side effect. To illustrate this, make the following changes to your program:

(a) Reinsert the CALL instruction (315) at location 003 011.
(b) Use timing bytes 377 377 in the time-delay subroutine.
(c) Alter the program steps from location 003 014 onward as in Fig. 4-10.

Reset the microcomputer and start your program. What do you observe?

```
003 014 076        MVIA     /LOAD ACCUMULATOR WITH
003 015 200        200      /A MODE CONTROL BYTE;
003 016 323        OUT      /AND OUTPUT IT
003 017 203        CNTRL    /TO THE CONTROL REGISTER
003 020 166        HLT
```

Fig. 4-10. Altered program steps.

We observed that the lamp monitor for bit PC0 was turned on and then, shortly thereafter, turned off. How can you explain this, when there was no bit-reset control byte in the program?

Any change to the control byte sent to the 8255, in which bit D7 is a logic 1, resets all of the bits at port C to logic 0s. Can you suggest why this feature is useful?

When a mode control byte is loaded into the PPI's control register, all of the bits of port C are *reset to logic 0*. This fact is useful since it defines the initial logic states of all the bits of port C, after the PPI has been initialized with a mode control byte. If an interface logic control line which is being driven must be initially at logic 0, then on the basis of the above feature, no further action is required following PPI initialization. If, on the other hand, the initial logic state of the interface control line is to be a logic 1, then the bit of port C which is driving the control line, must be set to logic 1 with a bit-set control byte following PPI initialization.

Questions

1. Using the mode control word format given in Fig. 2-2A, describe the way in which the PPI's ports A through C have been configured by the mode control word used in this experiment. Could port C have been configured for input in this experiment? If not, why not?

2. Explain why a control register device code of 203 was used in this experiment.

3. What advantage is to be gained by using the output of a mode control byte at the beginning of a program to reset the bits of port C?

4. Suggest some uses for the bit-set/reset feature of the 8255.

EXPERIMENT 4-2
A PPI-BASED DATA LOGGER

Purpose

The purpose of this experiment is to illustrate how the PPI bit-set/ reset feature can be used to generate pulses for circuit gating and reset operations. A simple mode 0 PPI-based *data logger* will be constructed.

Step 1

Wire the circuit shown in the schematic diagram of Fig. 4-12. Note that because a NAND gate was needed to gate the clock pulses through to the A_{IN} input of the first SN7493, the remainder of the gates in the SN7400 chip have been used to provide the inverters required in the circuit.

Step 2

Enter Program A into your microcomputer's read/write memory. Set the frequency of your external clock (connected to the SN7493 counters) to a value of from 1 to 5 Hz.

Programs (Fig. 4-11)

```
                    /
                    /PROGRAM "B"
                    /DESCRIPTION: THIS IS A PPI BASED DATA
                    /              LOGGING PROGRAM
                    /
                    DB MODE 202
                    DB CNTRL 203
                    DW DELAY 003 200
                    *003 000
003 000 061         LXISP
003 001 000         000
003 002 004         004
003 003 076         MVIA        /INITILISE PPI FOR MODE O WITH
003 004 202         MODE        /PORTS A&C=OUTPUT
                                /PORT B=INPUT
003 005 323         OUT
003 006 203         CNTRL
003 007 076         MVIA        /SET PCO TO ENABLE COUNTERS
003 010 001         001
003 011 323         OUT
003 012 203         CNTRL
003 013 076         MVIA        /OPEN GATE BY SETTING PC7
003 014 017         017
003 015 323         OUT
003 016 203         CNTRL
003 017 315         CALL        /WAIT WHILE A COUNT
003 020 200         DELAY       /IS COLLECTED
003 021 003         0
003 022 076         MVIA        /CLOSE GATE BY RESETTING PC7
003 023 016         016
003 024 323         OUT
003 025 203         CNTRL
003 026 333         IN          /INPUT DATA FROM
003 027 201         201         /PORT B
003 030 323         OUT         /OUTPUT DATA UNCHANGED TO
003 031 200         200         /PORT A
003 032 166         HLT

                    /
                    /PROGRAM "A"
                    /
                    /DESCRIPTION: THIS PROGRAM IS USED TO TEST THE
                    /SATISFACTORY OPERATION OF YOUR INTERFACE CIRCUIT
                    /
                    DB MODE 202
                    DB CNTRL 203
                    *003 000
003 000 076         MVIA        /SET UP MODE OF PPI FOR
003 001 202         MODE        /A=OUTPUT, B=INPUT
003 002 323         OUT         /C=OUTPUT
003 003 203         CNTRL
003 004 076         MVIA        /SET PCO TO LOGIC 1 TO
003 005 001         001         /ENABLE THE COUNTERS
003 006 323         OUT
003 007 203         CNTRL
003 010 076         MVIA        /OPEN GATE BY
003 011 017         017         /SETTING PC7
003 012 323         OUT
003 013 203         CNTRL
003 014 333   LOOP, IN          /INPUT COUNTS
003 015 201         201         /FROM PORT B
003 016 323         OUT         /OUTPUT IT TO
003 017 200         200         /PORT A
003 020 303         JMP
003 021 014         LOOP
003 022 003         0
```

Fig. 4-11. Program for Experiment 4-2.

Pin Configurations of Integrated-Circuit Chips (Fig. 4-12)

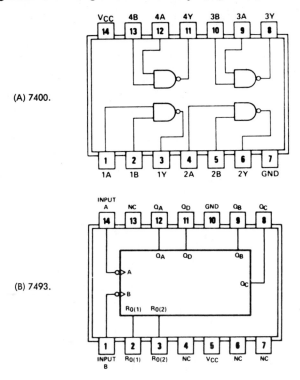

(A) 7400.

(B) 7493.

Fig. 4-12. IC chip pin configurations.

Step 3

Start the program. Do you note any changes at the LEDs that are connected to port A?

We observed a count that is incremented at the same rate as the clock that we set in Step 3. This is a checkout of your interface and your program. If you did not observe this, go back and check your program and your interface.

If you adjust your clock's frequency you should see a similar change in both the count at port A and in the rate at which the lamp monitors appear to be incremented.

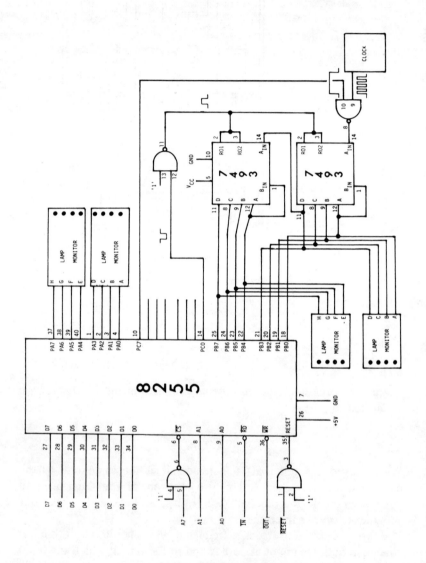

Fig. 4-13. Circuit for Experiment 4-2.

Step 4

Load Program B into memory. Study this program and the comments supplied, in conjunction with the circuit diagram, and draw a flow diagram of the program's operation in the space below. To help you, our comments are more generalized this time. You need not draw a flowchart of the DELAY subroutine. NOTE: If you have not completed Experiment 4-1, you will need to enter into memory the delay subroutine, DELAY, that is listed in Fig. 3-10.

As you will have seen by now, the object of the program is to log an 8-bit count of the number of pulses that passed through the SN7400 while the gate is open, and then to display this count at port A. The program first sets the SN7493 reset lines to 0 using PPI bit PC0. PPI bit PC7 is then set to logic 1 to open the gate and to allow pulse counting. Bit PC7 is reset to stop counting, the 8 bits of the two SN7493 counters are input and displayed at port A. The counters are reset by PC0.

Step 5

Set your external clock to a frequency of about 50–60 Hz. If you don't have an oscilloscope to do this, follow the steps below:

(a) Disconnect one lamp monitor from the PPI and reconnect the indicator to the clock's output. Adjust the clock frequency so that the flicker of the indicator is no longer seen.

(b) Reconnect the lamp monitor indicator to its proper pin on the 8255 chip.

Set the timing bytes in the DELAY subroutine as follows:

003 203 060 {These bytes will generate
003 204 165 }a 1-second delay.

Start your program. What do you observe on the two sets of lamp monitors?

We observed that the same counts were displayed at port A and on the lamp monitors connected to the SN7493 counters. Our count was 00111000_2, or 56_{10}. This value will probably be different to your observation since it depends upon your clock frequency. What does this count represent?

The count represents the number of pulses that the SN7493 counters detected during the time between when the gate was "opened" (step 003 016) and when it was "closed" (step 003 025). The DELAY subroutine kept the gate open for about 1 second.

Step 6

Repeat Step 5 again by running the program and note your count below. Is it close to the count in Step 5?

We again observed a count of 56_{10} on both the port A lamp monitors and on the lamp monitors connected to the SN7493 counters.

If the gate is set for 1 second, what function is the microcomputer performing?

It acts as a *frequency meter* since it detects and displays the number of pulses received per second and this, by definition, is the frequency of the pulse train from the external clock.

Step 7

Unfortunately, Program B only makes one measurement. Can the program be modified to make continuous measurements that can be used to update the display? Suggest simple changes to the program that will do this.

We changed the program so that after outputting the accumulated count to port A, the counters are reset and the program jumps to cycle through the appropriate steps again and again. The halt instruction (HLT) at location 003 032 was replaced with the instructions in Fig. 4-14.

Make the necessary changes to your program and try it. Do the displays indicate any changes in the clock's frequency when it is adjusted? They should! Remember though that the range of this frequency meter is 0 to 255 Hz.

```
003 032 076        MVIA     /RESET COUNTERS BY RESETTING
003 033 000        000      /PCO
003 034 323        OUT
003 035 203        CNTRL
003 036 303        JMP      /LOOP TO REPEAT THE
003 037 004        LOOP     /DATA LOGGING CYCLE
003 040 003        0
```

Fig. 4-14. Instructions replacing halt instruction.

Questions

1. How could you change your overall system to measure higher frequencies? (There is a hardware solution and a software solution to this problem.)

2. Why are the reset lines of the SN7493 counters driven through an inverter rather than being driven directly by PC0?

5

Status-Driven
Handshaking I/O:
Combined Mode 0 and
Bit-Set/Reset Operation

5-1. WHAT IS HANDSHAKING?

In Chapter 3 we discussed a classification of input/output operations into two categories, namely, unconditional and conditional data transfers. The unconditional data transfer is the simplest since it assumes that the I/O device is able to accept or supply data immediately upon request from the microcomputer. Conditional or asynchronous data transfers, which will be discussed in this chapter, are so called because of a basic lack of timing synchronization between a microprocessor and some of its peripherals. The data transfer is then "conditional" upon the peripheral being ready. Such timing difficulties arise in general because of the small, but finite, time required by many peripherals to either provide data upon request, or to accept and record data presented to them. Analog-to-digital (A/D) converters and paper tape readers, for example, both require a delay following the initiation of a read command before data is available for input. For the A/D converter, time is needed for the analog-to-digital conversion, while, for the paper tape reader, time is required to mechanically move the tape. A similar situation exists for output devices. A paper tape punch, for example, needs time to move and punch the tape, while a printer similarly needs time, after receipt of the data, to print the decoded character.

These I/O timing problems are overcome in practice by providing the peripherals with *status lines* which can be used to tell the microcomputer the current status of the I/O devices. These status lines or flags are generally in the form of flip-flops that indicate, among other things, whether the peripheral is *ready* for a data transfer or perhaps *busy* completing a previously initiated data transfer. On the microcomputer's part, it must be able to tell its peripherals when

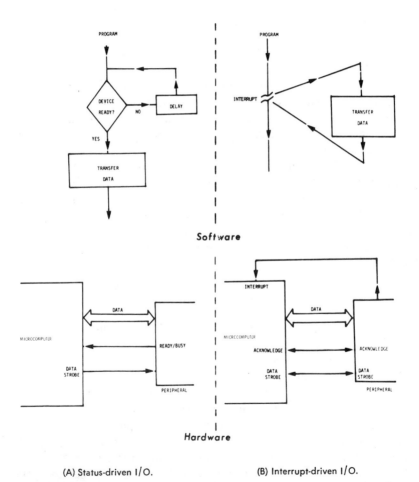

(A) Status-driven I/O.　　　　　(B) Interrupt-driven I/O.

Fig. 5-1. Essential differences between status-driven and interrupt-driven handshaking I/O.

it wants to initiate a data transfer. It does this by means of a *strobe pulse.*

In the simplest case, then, there are two control lines needed, in addition to the data lines, to interconnect a microcomputer and a "slow" peripheral. One line, the *strobe line,* is provided by the microcomputer while the second, the *busy/ready* line, is provided by the peripheral as shown in Fig. 5-1A. An orderly data flow between microcomputer and peripheral is then ensured by the exchange of pulses on these two lines. To read data from a peripheral, for example, the microcomputer sends a "data strobe" pulse down its strobe line to initiate the data conversion or data collection process. The peripheral responds with a "busy" logic level on its busy/ready line to indicate that it is fetching the data. The "busy" logic state is maintained by the peripheral until the data is available. Then the logic state changes to indicate that data is "ready." During the data conversion or collection period the microcomputer monitors the peripheral's busy/ready line, waiting for the logic change that indicates that data is ready. When the change is detected, the microcomputer then inputs data from the peripheral. This I/O procedure is illustrated in Fig. 5-1A.

The exchange of information between a microcomputer and a peripheral, in the form of pulses to synchronize data transfer, is analogous to the exchange of greetings between two persons by shaking each other's hands. Because of this similarity the use of busy/data-strobe flags in conditional data transfers is often called *handshaking* and the technique described as *handshaking I/O.*

5-2. STATUS-DRIVEN VERSUS INTERRUPT-DRIVEN HANDSHAKING I/O

Two types of handshaking I/O can be identified and are illustrated in Fig. 5-1. The first type is *status-driven handshaking I/O,* which was described above and supports a *BUSY/DATA-STROBE* interface. The problem with this type of handshaking I/O is that the microcomputer must wait in a delay loop for the peripheral to complete its data transfer or data conversion (see Fig. 5-1A). While this is acceptable in some dedicated microcomputer systems having a small number of peripherals, in larger systems, these delays, which may exceed 1 ms (millisecond), can be intolerable since they may prevent the microcomputer from completing other necessary data processing tasks.

The second type of handshaking I/O is *interrupt-driven handshaking I/O*. This overcomes the time-delay problem by allowing the microcomputer to proceed with its other processing tasks until a peripheral is ready to transfer data. At this time an interrupt pulse is generated by the interface and fed to the microcomputer's interrupt line as shown in Fig. 5-1B. This pulse causes the microcomputer to stop what it is doing and to service the cause of the interrupt, the peripheral. In this way the microcomputer is only committed to peripheral servicing for a short period when service is actually required. The topic of interrupts and interrupts servicing is difficult, and care must be taken to ensure that:

(i) The main program is not interrupted during the execution of essential code.

(ii) The appropriate service routine is quickly and easily located.

(iii) The status of the microcomputer at the time of an interrupt is preserved during interrupt servicing.

(iv) The system does not become interrupt bound, so that it spends all of its time servicing interrupting devices.

The PPI can be used in both modes 0 and 1 for unidirectional handshaking I/O. Mode 0 operation combined with the bit-set/reset feature of the PPI can be used to easily implement a status-driven handshaking I/O interface. Mode 1 operation has been designed for interrupt-driven handshaking I/O, and we will discuss this technique in Chapter 6.

5-3. IMPLEMENTING STATUS-DRIVEN HANDSHAKING I/O WITH A PPI

(A) Hardware

The status-driven handshaking I/O technique illustrated in Fig. 5-1A can be easily implemented in an 8080-based microcomputer by:

(i) Using the PPI in mode 0 operation for input and output of data and for the input of the peripheral's ready/busy status.

(ii) Using the PPI bit-set/reset feature of port C to generate the data strobe pulses.

Since many peripheral devices are designed for status-driven I/O, the PPI is often used to implement this type of handshaking technique, particularly where the inherent delays are unimportant.

Several important features of status-driven handshaking I/O can be identified and are illustrated in Fig. 5-1A:

- The *data strobe* pulse, whether for data input or data output, is *always* generated by the microcomputer and applied to the peripheral.
- The *ready/busy status* flag is always generated by the peripheral and must be read by the microcomputer.
- Data that is to be output must be latched and held by the microcomputer until the peripheral is ready to accept it. In mode 0 PPI operation, output data is latched at ports A, B, and C.
- Input data will usually be latched and held by the peripheral for some time after it indicates that data is ready.
- There is a great deal of CPU peripheral interaction during data transfer because of the need for the processor to regularly monitor the peripheral status line.

Fig. 5-2 shows the steps required to read data from a peripheral and write data to a peripheral, using a PPI-based status-driven handshaking I/O interface. In general, the peripheral data lines are connected to either port A or port B, which is then configured, using the mode control word for mode 0 input or output, as appropriate. The bits of port C are used for the handshaking control lines. The author recommends that, for standardization, the bits of port C upper, PC7–PC4, be used for data strobe lines and the bits of port C lower, PC3–PC0, be used to accept peripheral status lines. Port C upper would then be configured for mode 0 output and port C lower for mode 0 input. Fig. 5-3 illustrates this port allocation approach for the case of a paper tape punch and paper tape reader interfaced to the PPI for status-driven handshaking I/O.

(B) Software

Let us now look at subroutines that could be used to input data from the paper tape reader and output data to the paper tape punch, respectively. The first step, as usual though, is to initialize the PPI. In this case port A and port C upper must be configured for mode 0 output, and port B and port C lower must be configured for mode 0 input. Referring to the mode control word format shown in Fig. 2-2A, the required mode control word is 1 0000 011, or 203. As in the experiments of previous chapters where the PPI control lines $\overline{CS}$, A1, and A0 were similarly wired, the PPI device codes for ports

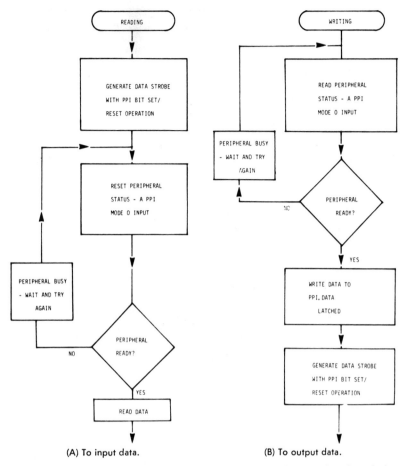

(A) To input data.   (B) To output data.

Fig. 5-2. Flow diagrams of the procedures required to input and output data through the PPI using status-driven handshaking I/O.

A through C and for the control register are 200, 201, 202, and 203, respectively.

Program 5-1 (Fig. 5-4)

The flow diagrams for the paper tape read and write subroutines were given in generalized form in Fig. 5-2. To provide an example of the programming techniques used with status-driven handshaking I/O, the paper punch subroutine has been written. The punch command input to the paper tape punch is an active high signal that moves the tape and initiates punching. This signal is actually the

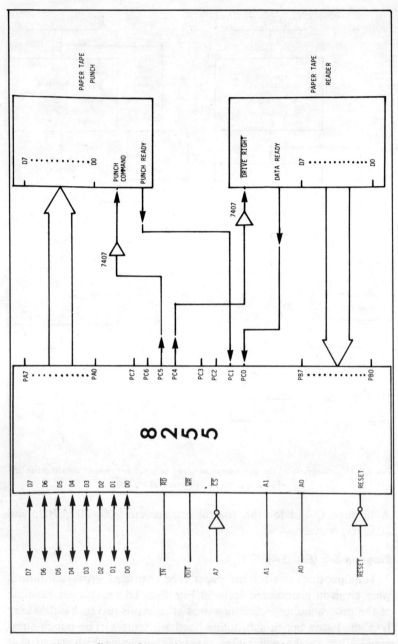

Fig. 5-3. PPI port allocation for interfacing a paper tape reader and paper tape punch for status-driven handshaking I/O.

paper tape punch *data strobe* signal, and it is wired to port C bit PC5. The bit-set/reset control words required to set and reset bit PC5, and therefore to set and reset the punch command input, can be constructed from Fig. 2-2B and are given in Table 5-1.

```
/
/THIS PROGRAM INITIALIZES THE PPI, INPUTS DATA FROM
/THE PAPER TAPE READER AND OUTPUTS IT TO THE PAPER
/TAPE PUNCH.
/
        MVIA    /LOAD A WITH THE PPI MODE
        MODE    /CONTROL WORD
        OUT     /OUTPUT MODE CONTROL WORD TO PPI
        CNTRL   /CONTROL REGISTER
        CALL    /INPUT A DATA BYTE FROM
        TAPEIN  /THE PAPER TAPE READER
        0
        CALL    /OUTPUT THE DATA BYTE TO
        TAPOUT  /PAPER TAPE PUNCH
        0
        HLT     /HALT
```

Fig. 5-4. Program 5-1.

The punch-ready output is an active high signal, which goes to a logic 1 to indicate that the punch is *ready* to accept data to be punched. A logic low on this line, which is wired to PC1, indicates

Table 5-1. Bit-Set/Reset Control Words Required to Set and Reset PC5 and PC4

Action	Symbol	Bit-Set/Reset Control Word
Set Drive Right (PC4)	PC4SET	1 000 100 1 = 211
Reset Drive Right (PC4)	PC4RST	1 000 100 0 = 210
Set Punch Command (PC5)	PC5SET	1 000 101 1 = 213
Reset Punch Command (PC5)	PC5RST	1 000 101 0 = 212

that the punch is *busy*. Our coding of the punch subroutine, following the flow diagram of Fig. 5-2B, is given below:

Subroutine Tapout (Fig. 5-5)

This program illustrates the standard masking technique that is used to determine the status of a peripheral. In this case the logic state of the bits at port C is determined by a port C input instruction. The logic state of bit PC1, which is wired to the "punch-ready" line, is then determined by a logical AND of the accumulator contents with a mask byte whose bits are set to 0 except for bit D1, which is set to a logic 1. If bit **PC1** is at logic 0 (punch busy), the result of the logical operation is 0. The "jump on zero result" (JZ) instruction will then cause the program to loop so that it will input the status of port **C** again for testing. If bit **PC1** is logic 1 (punch ready), the result of the logical operation is nonzero and the program does not loop, but it instead commences outputting a byte to the punch through port **A**.

This technique for testing a flag's status is a general one, and it can be used for the tape reader subroutine. Care must be taken when deciding on whether to use the JNZ or JZ instruction. The decision depends on the interpretation of the logic status of the peripheral's busy/ready flag. For the paper tape reader, its status line "Data

```
SUBROUTINE TAPOUT
     /DESCRIPTION: THIS SUBROUTINE OUTPUTS A DATA BYTE
     /            FROM THE ACCUMULATOR TO THE PAPER
     /            TAPE PUNCH
     /
          MOVBA    /SAVE BYTE TO BE OUTPUT
     LOOP, IN       /GET STATUS OF PUNCH
          PORTC
          ANI      /IS PUNCH BUSY?
          PC1MSK   /MASK BYTE 00 000 010
          JZ       /PC1="0". PUNCH BUSY SO
          LOOP     /LOOP & TRY AGAIN
          0
          MOVAB    /PC1="1", PUNCH READY SO
                   /RESTORE BYTE TO BE OUTPUT
          OUT      /OUTPUT BYTE TO PORT A
          PORTA
          MVIA     /LOAD A WITH "SET DATA STROBE"
          PC5SET   /CONTROL BYTE
          OUT      /SET DATA STROBE
          CNTRL
          DCRA     /GENERATE "RESET DATA STROBE" BYTE
          OUT      /RESET DATA STROBE
          CNTRL
          RET      /RETURN TO CALLER
```

Fig. 5-5. Subroutine tapout.

Ready" is again an active high flag with a logic 1 indicating that data is ready, and a logic 0 indicating that the reader is busy. Hence a JZ instruction would again be used with a mask byte 00 000 001. An exercise for you is to write the paper tape reader subroutine.

Remember that the generation of strobe pulses that are normally high or normally low is readily accomplished in software using the bit-set/reset feature of the PPI. This was discussed in Chapter 4. The "inversion" of the sense of a flag can also be accomplished easily in software through the appropriate choice of the JNZ instruction or the JZ instruction.

5-4. SUMMARY OF EXPERIMENT 5-1

Experiment   *Description*

5-1   The purpose of the experiment is to illustrate the technique of status-driven handshaking I/O using the mode 0 operation for the PPI. The experiment is in two parts:

             (a) Status-driven input operation.
             (b) Status-driven output operation.

          A circuit that can be used for both parts of the experiment is provided, and a program is given for the input operation. You are invited to write and test a subroutine to output data using status driven handshaking I/O. A subroutine is provided at the end of the experiment for comparison.

EXPERIMENT 5-1
STATUS-DRIVEN HANDSHAKING INPUT AND OUTPUT

Purpose

The aim of this experiment is to illustrate the technique of *status-driven I/O,* using both mode 0 PPI operation for input and output; and the PPI bit-set/reset operation for strobe pulse generation. The experiment is in two parts:

(a) Status-driven input operation.
(b) Status-driven output operation.

A circuit is provided for both parts, and a program is given for input operation. You may write and test a subroutine to output data using status-driven handshaking I/O. The requirements for this subroutine are given in Step 8. The author's subroutine is provided at the end of the experiment for comparison.

Status-Driven Input

Step 1

Wire the circuit shown in the schematic diagram of Fig. 5-8. In this circuit, port B is used to input data from logic switches. Port A is used to output data to a pair of SN7475 4-bit latches. Port C upper (PC7–PC4) is used to generate active-low strobe pulses with bit PC7 used via an inverter to enable the latches (the latches are enabled with a logic 1) and PC6 being used to supply the input strobe pulse. In this simple simulation of status driven handshaking I/O, the strobe pulse for data input is not physically required and so is used only to drive a lamp monitor. Port C lower (PC3–PC0)

Program (Fig. 5-6)

```
                    /
                    /STATUS DRIVEN I/O PROGRAM
                    /
                    DB MODE 203
                    DB CNTRL 203
                    DB PC7SET 017
                    DB PC6SET 015
                    DB PC6RST 014
                    *003 010
003 010 076              MVIA     /INITIALIZE PPI. PORT A & PORT C
003 011 203              MODE     /UPPER: O/P. PORT B & PORT C
                                  /LOWER: I/P
003 012 323              OUT
003 013 203              CNTRL
003 014 076              MVIA     /SET PC7, THE ACTIVE LOW
003 015 017              PC7SET   /STROBE FOR PORT A
003 016 323              OUT
003 017 203              CNTRL
003 020 076              MVIA     /SET PC6, THE ACTIVE LOW
003 021 015              PC6SET   /STROBE FOR PORT B
003 022 323              OUT
003 023 203              CNTRL
003 024 061              LXISP    /LOAD THE STACK
003 025 000              000      /POINTER
003 026 004              004
003 027 315     LOOP1,   CALL
003 030 042              READ
003 031 003              0
003 032 000              NOP
003 033 000              NOP
003 034 000              NOP
003 035 323              OUT      /OUTPUT ACCUMULATOR CONTENTS
003 036 000              000      /TO PORT 0
003 037 303              JMP
003 040 027              LOOP1
003 041 003              0
                    /
                    /SUBROUTINE:READ
                    /DESCRIPTION:THIS ROUTINE READS DATA FROM
                    /PORT B USING STATUS DRIVEN HANDSHAKING I/O
                    /
003 042 365     READ,    PUSHPSW  /SAVE PROGRAM STATUS
                                  /WORD & ACCUMULATOR CONTENTS
003 043 076              MVIA     /GENERATE AN ACTIVE
003 044 014              PC6RST   /LOW STROBE PULSE
003 045 323              OUT
003 046 203              CNTRL
003 047 315              CALL     /GENERATE A DELAY SO THAT
003 050 200              DELAY    /THE STROBE PULSE CAN BE SEEN
003 051 003              0
```

Fig. 5-6. Program for

has been assigned as input for the BUSY/READY status of the input device at port B (PC2) and the output device at port A (PC3).

Schematic Diagram of Circuit (Fig. 5-8)

From this data and using the mode control word format of Fig. 2-2A, construct the mode control word that is required to configure the PPI as shown in Fig. 5-7. Use the bit-set/reset control word format of Fig. 2-2B to construct bit-set/reset control words which will

```
003 052 074            INRA
003 053 323            OUT
003 054 203            CNTRL
003 055 333   LOOP2,   IN      /INPUT BUSY/READY STATUS FROM
003 056 202            202     /PORT C
003 057 346            ANI
003 060 004            004     /MASK BYTE FOR PORT C BIT PC2
003 061 302            JNZ     /PC2='1'. THEREFORE, PORT B IS
003 062 100            POINTX  /READY. JUMP INPUT DATA
003 063 003            0
003 064 016            MVIC    /PC2='0'. THEREFORE PORT B IS
003 065 005            005     /BUSY, SO GENERATE
003 066 015   LOOP3,   DCRC    /A DELAY
003 067 315            CALL
003 070 200            DELAY
003 071 003            0
003 072 302            JNZ
003 073 066            LOOP3
003 074 003            0
003 075 303            JMP     /NOW TRY PORT B
003 076 055            LOOP2   /STATUS AGAIN
003 077 003            0
003 100 333   POINTX,  IN
003 101 201            201
003 102 107            MOVBA   /SAVE CONTENTS OF PORT B
003 103 361            POPPSW
003 104 311            RET

              /SUBROUTINE: DELAY
              /DESCRIPTION: THIS SUBROUTINE GENERATES A ONE SECOND
              /             DELAY FOR A MICROCOMPUTER HAVING A
              /             750KHZ CLOCK
              /
              *003 200
003 200 365   DELAY,   PUSHPSW
003 201 325            PUSHD
003 202 021            LXID    /LOAD TIMING BYTES FOR
003 203 000            000     /A ONE SECOND DELAY
003 204 200            200
003 205 033   LOOP4,   DCXD
003 206 173            MOVAE
003 207 262            ORAD
003 210 302            JNZ
003 211 205            LOOP4
003 212 003            0
003 213 321            POPD
003 214 361            POPPSW
003 215 311            RET
```

Experiment 5-1.

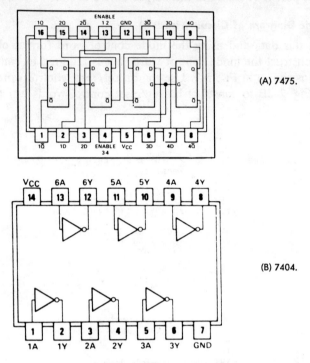

(A) 7475.

(B) 7404.

Fig. 5-7. IC chip pin configurations.

set and reset bits **PC7** and **PC6** of port **C**. Write your results in the space provided.

The required results are as follows:

Mode control word byte: 1 0000 011 or 203 (MODE)
Bit-set/reset word bytes:
    PC7 set: 0 000 111 1 or 017 (PC7SET)
    PC7 reset: 0 000 111 0 or 016 (PC7RST)
    PC6 set: 0 000 110 1 or 015 (PC6SET)
    PC6 reset: 0 000 110 0 or 014 (PC6RST)

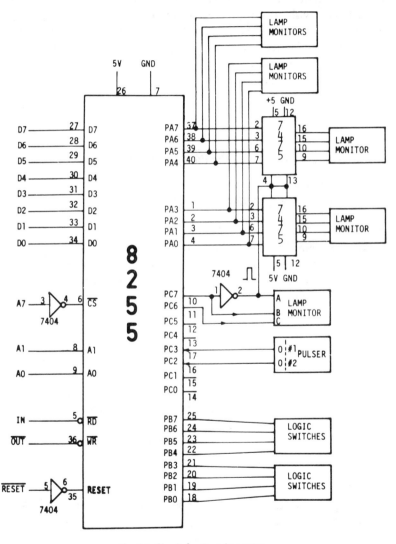

Fig. 5-8. Circuit for Experiment 5-1.

Note how these bytes are used in the program to initialize the PPI and generate the port A strobe pulse.

Step 2

Load the program into memory. Study the program listing. You will see that it is divided into a main program section and a port B read subroutine. In this first part of the experiment we will be concerned only with status-driven reading. In the space below, sketch a flowchart of the program. Your flowchart of the read subroutine should be similar to that given in Fig. 5-2A. Note any differences you find in the space below.

The two differences are that the data which is input through port B is:

(i) output to port 0; and
(ii) saved in register B of the 8080A.

Step 3

Set the logic switches to 1010 1010. Execute the program, commencing at location 003 010 while watching output port 0 and the lamp monitors that are connected to PC7 and PC6. Describe and explain what you observe.

We observed that the lamp monitor which is wired to bit PC6 of port C was turned off for approximately 1 second. There was no change in the contents of port 0. The program has entered the READ subroutine which generates a 1-second active-low pulse at bit PC6 of port C. It is now polling bit PC2 for the busy/ready status of port B.

Step 4

Now press pulser B for at least 3 seconds and then release it. What do you observe at port 0?

We observed that the data byte, 252, which was set on the logic switches, was output to port 0. Since pulser B is the BUSY/READY status flag for port B, what conclusion can be drawn concerning the logic states which represent the BUSY status and the READY status of the "peripheral" at port B?

Since the pulser is normally in a logic 0 state and goes to logic 1 only when it is pressed, the program interprets a logic 1 as the READY status of port B.

Step 5

Set the logic switches to 1111 0000. Now press and release pulser B as quickly as you can. Do you observe any change to the byte which is displayed at port 0? If not, why not?

We found that, on most occasions, no change was observed in the byte displayed at port 0. The reason for this is that the program was not monitoring the port B status flag during the time that the pulser was pressed. It was, in fact, looping through the instructions within LOOP3 of the program that generate a 4-second delay.

The monitoring of a status flag is known as "polling" and this step was included to illustrate a potential problem which may arise if the status flag is not checked often enough. The solution to the problem is to poll the status flag more often. Hence, remove the call instruction at location 003 067 by inserting NOPs (000) into memory locations 067, 070, and 071 (LO address bytes). This will reduce the delay to virtually zero. Now, alter the logic switches and press and release pulser B. Repeat the operation with different bytes at the logic switches. Do you observe that the byte at port B was read each time? We did.

Step 6

Press and release pulser A. What do you observe, if anything? Why?

We observed no change at port 0. Pulser A represents the BUSY/ READY status flag for port A which has been configured for data output. It is not checked by the READ subroutine.

Step 7

Insert into LO memory locations 032 and 033 the following bytes:

```
003 032   326   SUI
003 033   060   060
```

Set the logic switches to 066 (ASCII for decimal 6). Execute the program and press and release pulser B. What byte is displayed at port 0? Why?

The byte 006 was displayed at port 0 when we ran the program and pressed and released the pulser. The READ subroutine input the byte 066 from port B when the pulser was pressed. This is the value in the accumulator when the instruction, which we inserted above, is exceuted following the return from the READ subroutine. Since 006 is the value for decimal 6, in what way has the mirco-computer processed the data from port B?

As ASCII to BCD conversion has been done by the microcomputer. This is a very useful technique since the ASCII codes for the decimal numbers 0 to 9 are 060 through 071, respectively. Hence, set the ASCII code for 8 (070) on your logic switches and have the micro-computer convert this to BCD at port 0 by pressing and releasing the pulser. Did it work? It did for us.

Status-Driven Output

Step 8

You are now invited to write a subroutine, WRITE, using the flowchart of Fig. 5-2B. The subroutine is to output data, *stored in register B,* to port A using status-driven mode 0 PPI operation. The program should commence at location 003 120. Bit PC7 (see sche-

```
          DB CNTRL 203
          DB PC7RST 017
          *003 120
          /
          /SUBROUTINE:WRITE
          /DESCRIPTION:THIS SUBROUTINE OUTPUTS DATA
          /HELD IN REGISTER B,TO PORT A USING STATUS
          /DRIVEN HANDSHAKING I/O.
          /
003 120 365   WRITE,   PUSHPSW
003 121 333   LOOP2,   IN       /INPUT BUSY/READY STATUS
003 122 202            202      /FROM PORT C
003 123 346            ANI
003 124 010            010      /MASK BYTE FOR PORT C BIT PC3
003 125 312            JZ       /PC3='0'. PORT A BUSY, TRY
003 126 121            LOOP2    /AGAIN
003 127 003            0
003 130 170            MOVAB    /PORT A READY, RESTORE DATA TO
                                /BE OUTPUT
003 131 323            OUT      /OUTPUT DATA TO PORT A
003 132 200            200
003 133 076            MVIA     /GENERATE ACTIVE LOW STROBE PULSE
003 134 017            PC7RST
003 135 323            OUT
003 136 203            CNTRL
003 137 074            INRA
003 140 323            OUT
003 141 203            CNTRL
003 142 361            POPPSW
003 143 311            RET
```

Fig. 5-9. WRITE subroutine.

matic diagram of circuit) is an *active-low* strobe and the BUSY/
READY status flag for port A is to be input at port C bit PC3 with
the convention that a logic 1 represents the READY status. Since
the accumulator contents and the logic state of the zero flag will be
destroyed during the execution of the WRITE subroutine, don't
forget to push the program status word (PUSH PSW) on to the stack
at the beginning of the routine and pop it off the stack immediately
prior to the return statement. (See Fig. 5-9 for comparison.)

Having written the subroutine, you may incorporate it into the
program by inserting a CALL instruction at location 003 032 as
follows:

```
          003 032  315  CALL
          003 033  120  WRITE
          003 034  003   0
```

If the program is now run commencing at location 003 010, data
should be input from port B and output to port A when pulsers B
and A respectively are pressed. The data which is monitored at port
0 in steps 3 through 7 can now be displayed on the lamp monitors at
port A of the PPI by pressing pulser A.

6

Interrupt-Driven
Handshaking I/O:
Mode 1 Operation of the PPI

6-1. INTRODUCTION

The mode 1 operation of the PPI was designed to permit conditional data transfers between the 8080A and its peripherals without the microcomputer having continuously to poll the status of its peripherals in the manner illustrated in Chapter 5. Polling of peripheral status is clearly an inefficient use of the 8080A's capability in many cases. The role of the PPI in mode 1 operation is to *manage* microcomputer peripheral data transfers using handshaking signals and to *interrupt* the microcomputer only when it is absolutely required. The microcomputer is thus freed for other logic sequencing and data processing tasks.

Fig. 6-1 illustrates schematically the way in which the 8255 can be used in mode 1 operation for data input and data output. In this example the input device is a fully decoded keyboard and the output device is a video display.

The important feature of this mode 1 interface, which distinguishes it from the busy/data-strobe status-driven interface in Fig. 5-3, is that *interrupts are used* to signal the microcomputer that a data transfer between the PPI and the peripherals has been completed.

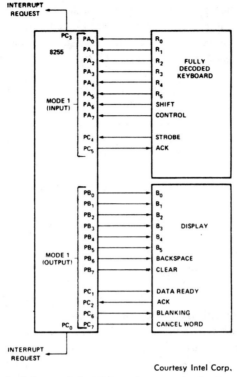

Courtesy Intel Corp.

Fig. 6-1. An example of the use of the PPI in mode 1 operation for data input and output.

The handshaking signals are also slightly different from those used in Fig. 5-3. In Fig. 6-1 data strobe/acknowledge signals are used. The *data strobe* signal is generated by the device from which the data originates. The receiving device then signals the sender that it has accepted the data by raising its *acknowledge* flag (ACK for both peripherals in Fig. 6-1). When a key is pressed, and the appropriate code is available at the data lines R0 to R5 for input to the microcomputer, the keyboard generates a "strobe" signal which the PPI acknowledges when the microcomputer has read the data from port A. Similarly, when the PPI has a data byte ready at port A for output to the video display, the PPI generates a pulse on the "data ready" line of the video display to signal it that data is available for display. When the display has latched the byte, it acknowledges receipt of the byte by pulsing the ACK line. In contrast, the two data strobe signals used in Fig. 5-3 were generated by the PPI to request data transfer with the peripherals.

The difference between the busy/data strobe and the data strobe/ acknowledge handshaking signals is then essentially one of where the *initiative* for the data transfer lies. For a busy/data strobe-based interface, the initiative lies with the microcomputer for both input and output. For a data strobe/acknowledge-based interface, the initiative always lies with the device from which the data originates. This may be the microcomputer (through the PPI) or the peripheral as illustrated in Fig. 5-1B. Because of this the data strobe/acknowledge handshaking signals are better suited to the mode 1 operation of the PPI where the PPI manages the data transfers independently of the microcomputer. We will now look in more detail at the features of the PPI when it is configured for mode 1 operation.

6-2. MODE 1 PPI FEATURES

The allocation of the PPI's 24 interface lines for mode 1 operation is shown schematically in Fig. 6-2. Ports A and B are used for unidirectional handshaking I/O, and port C provides the required control lines. Each mode 1 port (A or B) consists of an 8-bit data port, three control lines, and some internal interrupt support logic. This leaves two free port C lines that are available for mode 0 I/O or pulse generation using the PPI bit-set/reset features. Each mode 1 8-bit data port (port A or B) can be used for either input or output operations, and both inputs and outputs are latched. In Fig. 6-2 the data lines and the control or handshaking lines, associated with each mode 1 port, have been bracketed. Notice that the two free I/O lines have been grouped with the port A control lines. The reason is that, in mode 2 operation of the PPI, port A is used for bidirectional handshaking I/O and it uses all five port C bits (PC7 to PC3) as control lines. Notice also that the allocation of the port A and port B control lines changes for input and output. Let us look first at the input control lines to see how these are used to control mode 1 input operation.

(A) Mode 1 Input

The internal control and external handshaking signals used to control mode 1 input operations at ports A and B are illustrated in Fig. 6-3.

Each port has three external handshaking signals ($\overline{STB}$, IBF, and INTR) and one internal control line (INTE). These are defined as follows:

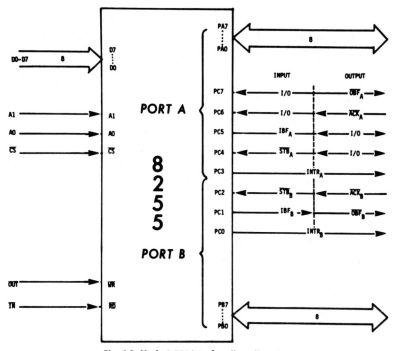

Fig. 6-2. Mode 1 PPI interface line allocation.

- $\overline{STB}$ (*Strobe Input*). This is the *data strobe* signal, which indicates that the peripheral has data ready for input. It must be generated by an external peripheral. Port C bits PC4 and PC2 are used, and a logic 0 on these inputs will load data into the input latches of either port A or port B respectively (*cf* PC4 in Fig. 6-1).

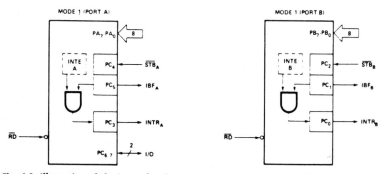

Fig. 6-3. Illustration of the internal and external control signals required to manage mode 1 PPI input operation.

- *IBF* (*Input Buffer Full*). This is the PPI's *acknowledge* signal for data that has been input to the PPI from a peripheral. A logic 1 on this output indicates that data has been loaded into the port A (PC5) or port B (PC1) input latch. The line is set to a logic 1 approximately 300 ns after the $\overline{STB}$ input goes to logic 0.

- *INTR* (*Interrupt Request*). As its name suggests, this signal can be used to interrupt the 8080A when data from an external peripheral has been loaded into the port A or port B latches for input to the 8080A. This interrupt request output is set to logic 1 if $\overline{STB}$, IBF, and INTE, the internal control line, are all at logic 1.

- *INTE* (*Interrupt Enable*). This is an internal, interrupt control flip-flop that can be used to inhibit (INTE = 0) or enable (INTE = 1) the generation of interrupts, from either port A or port B. The logic state of INTE is set or reset using the bit-set/reset function of port C. The interrupt enable flip-flop of port A, INTE A, is controlled by the setting and resetting of PC4, while INTE B, the interrupt enable flip-flop for port B, is controlled by the setting and resetting of PC2. It should be noted that, in mode 1 operation, the bit-set/reset operations on PC4 and PC2 to control the INTE flip-flops of port A and port B respectively, are internal PPI operations and have no effect on the logic states of PPI pins PC4 and PC2, which for mode 1 data input are used as *strobe input* ($\overline{STB}$) lines. The advantage of the internal PPI INTE flip-flops is that they permit the microcomputer user to selectively disable peripherals under software control. This is an extremely useful facility to have available in circumstances where it is known, for example, that at certain times, all the microcomputer processing capability will be required for one important task (data processing, I/O, etc.). System resource priority can be shifted in this way to meet peak demands.

Fig. 6-4 shows a timing diagram for the mode 1 input which we can use to gain an appreciation of the operating sequence for mode 1 input. The mode 1 data input operation is initiated by an active low *strobe* input ($\overline{STB}$) pulse from a peripheral which causes the *input buffer full* (IBF) output line to go to logic 1. This signal can be used as a PPI acknowledge signal. The logic 1 indicates that data has been loaded into the input latch of the port, but that it has not yet been read by the microcomputer. The next step depends on the status of the interrupt enable (INTE) flip-flop for the port. If this had been previously set using the port C bit-set/reset feature, the PPI's interrupt request line (INTR) will be set to logic 1 when $\overline{STB}$ returns to a logic 1. If INTE was at logic 0, INTR will not be set when $\overline{STB}$ returns to a logic 1 and the data from the peripheral is effectively lost. Assuming that INTE was set, the resulting logic 1 on the interrupt request line (INTR) can be used to interrupt the microcomputer. The microcomputer must then determine which port

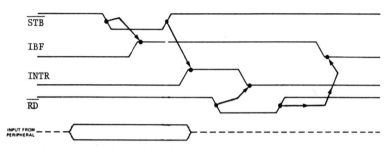

Fig. 6-4. Mode 1 input timing diagram. INTE is assumed to be at logic 1.

is interrupting it, either by using a vectored interrupt or by polling. Having done this it then reads the data that is held in the PPI's input port latch. The logic 0 that is generated on the $\overline{RD}$ line during the microcomputer read operation, resets INTR back to a logic 0. The IBF line is reset to 0 by the trailing edge of $\overline{RD}$ and hence the PPI acknowledges to the peripheral that the microcomputer system has received the data. The mode 1 data input operation is then complete.

The advantage of this input procedure is that an input device can request service from the microcomputer simply by strobing its data into port A or port B. It is the PPI which manages the input operation and the microcomputer is only interrupted when data is actually ready to be input from the PPI.

(B) Mode 1 Output

The internal control and external handshaking signals used to control mode 1 output operations are illustrated in Fig. 6-5. Three external handshaking signals ($\overline{OBF}$, $\overline{ACK}$, and INTR) and the interrupt enable (INTE) internal control signal are used to manage mode 1 output operations at ports A and B, and these signals are defined as follows:

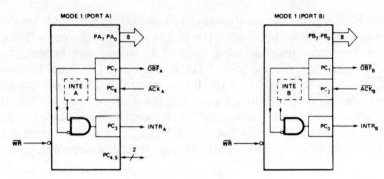

Fig. 6-5. Illustration of the internal and external control signals required to manage mode 1 PPI output operation.

- $\overline{OBF}$ (*Output Buffer Full*). This is the *output data strobe signal* and is generated by the PPI. A logic 0 on this line indicates that the microcomputer has written data to the port, and that the data has been latched.
- $\overline{ACK}$ (*Acknowledge Input*). A logic 0 on this input line indicates that the peripheral has accepted data from the port's output lines. It is an acknowledge signal from the peripheral.
- INTR (*Interrupt Request*). This output line is used to interrupt the microcomputer after data has been output by the PPI, and accepted by the peripheral. INTR is set to logic 1, when $\overline{ACK}$, $\overline{OBF}$, and INTE are all at logic 1, to indicate that the data has been received by the peripheral.
- INTE (*Interrupt Enable*). This is the interrupt enable flip-flop as described for mode 1 input. As for input operations the $INTE_A$ and $INTE_B$ flip-flops can again be used to selectively enable or disable ports A and B respectively, this time for mode 1 output. For PPI output operations $INTE_A$ is controlled by setting and resetting PC6, while $INTE_B$ is controlled by setting and resetting PC2. Note again that the bit-set/reset operations on PC6 and PC2 for mode 1 output are operations on *internal PPI flip-flops*. The logic states of the PPI's pins PC6 and PC2 are unaffected. In mode 1 output these PPI pins are used for the $\overline{ACK}$ inputs from the external peripherals.

Fig. 6-6 shows a timing diagram which illustrates the operating sequence for a mode 1 output operation. The initial write operation at program start-up will probably be initiated by the CPU, while the INTR line is at logic 0. After this, interrupt-driven operation, as

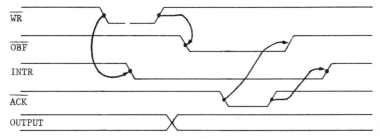

Fig. 6-6. Timing diagram for mode 1 output operation. The interrupt enable (INTE) flip-flop is assumed to have been set to logic 1.

illustrated in the timing diagram of Fig. 6-6, will be established. Let us assume that interrupt driven mode 1 output operation has been established at either port A or port B. That is to say, a previously initiated write operation to a peripheral has been acknowledged, setting INTR to logic 1. This is the point at which we can consider the timing diagram in Fig. 6-6 to commence. Through the use of a vectored interrupt or through polling, the CPU must then identify the interrupting port and initiate a new write sequence to the PPI mode 1 output port. The leading edge of WR (Fig. 6-6) resets INTR to logic 0, removing the CPU interrupt.* The rising of WR causes $\overline{OBF}$ to go low, which, in turn, strobes the data on the output port lines into the peripheral latches. When the peripheral has accepted the data, it sets $\overline{ACK}$, the peripheral line, low, and this resets $\overline{OBF}$ to logic 1. When $\overline{ACK}$ returns to logic one, the interrupt request line, INTR, is set to a logic 1. The CPU is then interrupted and another cycle is initiated.

In summary, a model 1 write sequence is initiated by an interrupt. The CPU write operation causes a data strobe pulse ($\overline{OBF}$) to be generated by the PPI, strobing data to the peripheral. The peripheral acknowledges receipt of this data by driving $\overline{ACK}$ low. Following the $\overline{ACK}$ pulse another interrupt is generated to initiate a new write operation.

(C) Input/Output Mode 1 Combinations

Because ports A and B can be assigned independently for input or output, two mode 1 input/output combinations are possible as shown in Fig. 6-7. Our initial example (Fig. 6-1) of the use of the PPI in mode 1 operation for combined data input and output can

---

* This should *not* be confused with an interrupt acknowledge.

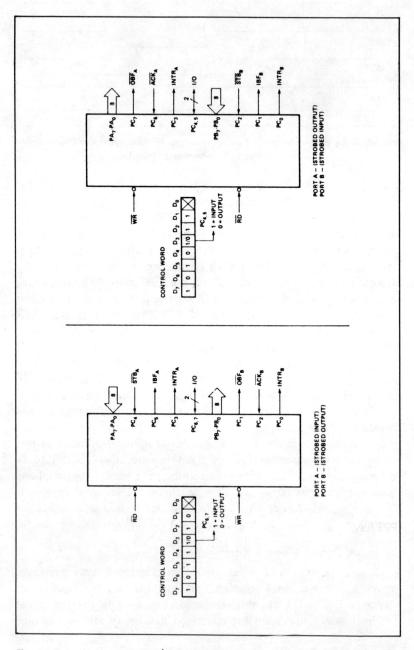

Fig. 6-7. Port A and port B input/output combinations for mode 1 operation of the PPI.

now be compared with Fig. 6-7A to see the way in which the port C control bits have been used. Notice that the two PPI port C lines (PC6 and PC7) that are not used for handshaking have to be used to drive the blanking and cancel word flags. These lines would be set and reset using the port C bit-set/reset feature.

6-3. MODE 1 OPERATING REQUIREMENTS

(A) Hardware

In most microcomputer applications the peripherals are selected on the basis of cost and overall system requirements. The task of interfacing these peripherals to the CPU must then be tackled, and it is here that the PPI is most valuable because of its flexibility. If the peripherals to be used in a microcomputer application support a data strobe/acknowledge interface of mode 1 type PPI operation, the *first hardware decision* that must be made, in implementing the mode 1 interface, is whether port A and port B are to be used for input, output, or a combination of both. Once this decision is made, the port C handshaking signals are automatically defined (*cf* Fig. 6-2), and the appropriate data strobe and acknowledge bits can be connected to the peripherals.

The *second hardware decision* which must be made is the type of interrupt structure that will be used, that is, a vectored interrupt or a polled interrupt. The *vectored interrupt* generally results in a faster CPU response to the interrupting peripheral, since CPU operation is automatically vectored to the correct service routine by one of the 8080's single-byte call or restart instructions, RST. An additional three-state buffer latch such as the SN74365 is required to "jam" the RST instruction into the 8080A's instruction register when the CPU acknowledges the interrupt with a logic low on the interrupt acknowledge ($\overline{INTA}$ or $\overline{IACK}$) output. Fig. 6-8 illustrates one circuit that can be used to implement vectored interrupts with a PPI having an input device at port A and an output device at port B. Notice that we have used the IBF and $\overline{OBF}$ signals as inputs to the SN74365. It is worth noting here that the circuit will not support simultaneous interrupts and that priority in servicing the interrupts must be set in the software.

Referring now to the mode 1 input and output timing diagrams of Fig. 6-4 and 6-6 respectively, it will be seen that both IBF and $\overline{OBF}$ are logic high during the time that $INTR_A$ and $INTR_B$ are high. Hence in this example the vectored interrupt RESTART in-

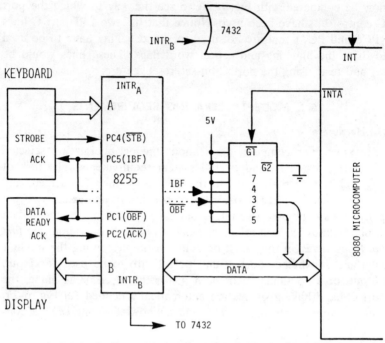

Fig. 6-8. Circuit diagram of a vector-interrupt mode 1 PPI interface to an 8080A-based microcomputer.

structions RST 7(377) and RST 5(357) would be generated for input and output respectively. Note also that because the 8080A has only one interrupt line (INT), the INTR$_A$ and INTR$_B$ signals have been ORed together and the resulting output wired to INT.

If only one port is required for mode 1 I/O, a feature of the 8228 system controller chip can be effectively used to jam an RST 7 vector interrupt instruction into the 8080A instruction register during an interrupt. All that is required is to wire the 8228 $\overline{\text{INTA}}$ line to +12 V through a 1-kΩ resistor. This then avoids the need for the SN74365 three-state buffer shown in Fig. 6-8. In microcomputer systems that do not use an 8228 an RST 7 code (377), should be established using an SN74365 as in Fig. 6-8 but with all its input lines connected to logic 1.

If two or more mode 1 ports are used in an interrupt-driven interface, an RST 7 instruction alone can still be employed, if the mode 1 ports are then checked or polled to determine which one is requesting service. This is the *polled interrupt* approach. The ques-

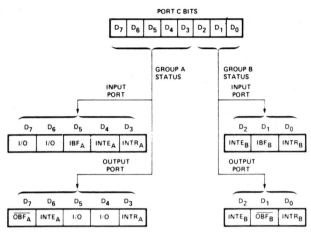

Fig. 6-9. The mode 1 status word, which is obtained by reading port C.

tion then arises as to how the status of each mode 1 port can be determined, since this point was not mentioned earlier. The answer is to initiate a read operation from port C. When this is done and the 8255 is configured for mode 1 operation, the microcomputer will receive the *mode 1 status word,* which is shown in Fig. 6-9. The status of the INTR lines (bits D3 and D0) can then be checked by software since the bits in the status word represent, in general, the state of the associated ports C lines. By comparing the mode 1 status word in Fig. 6-9 with the port C pin allocation for input and output shown in Fig. 6-2, you will see that the only differences are the replacement in Fig. 6-9 of:

(a) The $\overline{\text{STB}}$ lines (PC4 and PC2) by the INTE flip-flop status for input.
(b) The $\overline{\text{ACK}}$ lines (PC6 and PC2) by the INTE flip-flop status for output.

The polled interrupt approach requires more software to determine which port was interrupting. It therefore has an inherently slower service response time which is still, however, only on the order of a few tens of microseconds.

(B) Software

The first step in writing software for mode 1 PPI operation is to write the *PPI initialization* code that will configure the PPI as was decided from consideration from the hardware. This is done by

133

loading the accumulator with the appropriate mode control byte and outputting it to the PPI control register. The mode control byte is determined in the usual way by referring to the mode control word format of Fig. 2-2A. Note that in this case bits D6, D5, and D2 are set to 0, 1, and 1, respectively, in order to set ports A and B to mode 1.

The second PPI mode 1 initialization operation is to set the interrupt enable INTE flip-flops using the port C bit-set/reset feature. Care should be taken to ensure that the correct bits are set since *the port C bits assigned for the INTE flags of ports A and B change for input and output* (*cf* Fig. 6-9). Port C bits PC4 and PC2 are allocated for mode 1 input, and bits PC6 and PC2 are allocated for mode 1 output INTE flip-flops.

The remaining software associated with mode 1 PPI input/output operations is concerned with servicing the interrupts ($INTR_A$ and $INTR_B$) generated by port A and port B. The software requirements of polled interrupt and vectored interrupt handshaking I/O are illustrated, and may be compared, in Fig. 6-10. In general, more steps are required to service polled interrupt handshaking I/O, since at each interrupt the mode 1 status word must be read, and the status of the port A and B INTR lines (*cf* bits D0 and D3 of Fig. 6-9) must be separately checked to determine which port is requesting service. The programming technique used to determine the status of a port is the same as that which was used in Chapter 5 to determine peripheral status (*cf* Section 5-3B), i.e., masking combined with a program jump based upon the results of a logical AND of the status byte and the masking byte. This technique is illustrated in the example that is described in Section 6-4. The response speed of a polled-interrupt handshaking I/O subroutine can be improved in circumstances where it is known that one peripheral will require service more often than others. In such cases it is clearly most efficient to check the status of the more demanding peripheral first. The port whose status is checked first in a program is said to have highest *priority*. When writing polled interrupt software the priority of the system's peripherals must be decided upon so that the status of each port can be checked in the most appropriate order. Such decisions can be made on the basis of response speed or perhaps on the basis of some other criterion such as the relative importance of the data from one or all of the peripherals.

The software for vectored interrupts as shown in Fig. 6-10B is much simpler than for polled interrupts and only involves writing

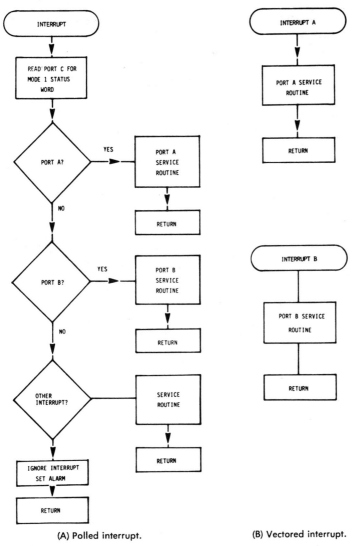

(A) Polled interrupt.　　　　　(B) Vectored interrupt.

Fig. 6-10. Flow diagrams of the interrupt subroutines needed to support polled-interrupt and vectored-interrupt mode 1 operation of the PPI.

the service routines for each port at the appropriate vector restart location. Because of this simplicity of programming, the peripheral service response time is quicker than for polled-interrupt handshaking I/O. It is useful with vectored interrupts to again consider the servicing priority of the peripherals. In this case, however, servicing priority will, in general, be set in hardware rather than software, and this is discussed in Unit 23 of *Introductory Experiments in Digital Electronics and 8080A Microcomputer Programming and Interfacing,* Book 2. A circuit which establishes peripheral service priority in hardware using an SN74148 priority encoder is also discussed in that unit.

In microcomputer systems where CPU data processing and logic sequencing requirements are minimal the *continuous polling* of the PPI's INTR status lines may be acceptable. Flow diagrams of the software required to support continuous polling for read and write I/O operations are shown in Fig. 6-11. A small advantage of this approach is that no external hardware other than the PPI is needed.

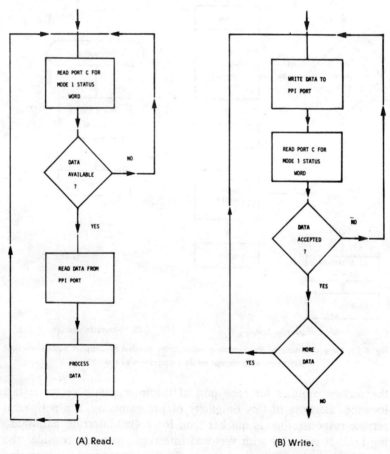

(A) Read.   (B) Write.

Fig. 6-11. Flow diagrams for continuous software-polled mode 1 PPI operation.

6-4. AN EXAMPLE

To illustrate the considerations involved in using mode 1 PPI operation, let us look at the example in Fig. 6-1. Here a fully decoded keyboard and a video display have been interfaced to a PPI. We will look at the hardware and then the software considerations.

(A) Hardware

In producing the schematic of Fig. 6-1 a number of important decisions have already been made. Clearly both peripherals support a data strobe/acknowledge interface and so it was decided to use mode 1 operation of the PPI. The spare I/O lines of port C were then allocated to the video display as control lines. These decisions were made in tailoring the PPI to the peripheral requirements. Having decided to employ an interrupt-driven system rather than a continuous software polled system, the next problem is to decide between the vector-interrupt and the polled-interrupt approaches. The decision will usually be made on the basis of the required service response speed and the tradeoff between additional hardware and extra software. The author recommends that if maximum response speed is not necessary and if memory space is not at a premium, then the polled interrupt approach be adopted since it reduces the external hardware to an interrupt instruction port and a single OR gate. This is the approach that we will use.

The required interface circuit is shown in Fig. 6-8 with the SN74365 hard-wired for a 367 (RST 6) vector. Because a polled-interrupt approach is being used the servicing priority of the peripherals will be determined by the software rather than the hardware. We will assign the highest priority to the display since it will require refreshing more often than the entry of data at the keyboard. Finally, the decision to use port A for input and port B for output is quite arbitrary.

(B) Software

The first requirement when writing the software is to draw a flow diagram. Fig. 6-10A shows the flow diagram for the polled interrupt software. We will not flowchart the port A and B service routines since these are a function of the particular microcomputer system used for the keyboard and display. Before coding the polled-interrupt flowchart however, we must first write the PPI initialization code. This is shown in the program listing of Fig. 6-12 together

```
                   *000 060
000 060 303         JMP     /JUMP TO VECTOR RESTART
000 061 060         RESTRT  /SUBROUTINE
000 062 003         0
                   /       .
                   /       .
                   /       .
                   /       .
                   /
                   /PROGRAM STARTS HERE
                   /
                   DB MODE 264
                   DB PORTC 202
                   DB CNTRL 203
                   DB INTEAS 011
                   DB INTEBS 005
                   DB MASKA 010
                   DB MASKB 001
                   DW PASVC 003 300
                   DW PBSVC 003 200
                   *003 001
003 001 076 START,  MVIA    /INITIALIZE PPI-PORT A:MODE 1
003 002 264         MODE    /INPUT; PORT B:MODE 1 OUTPUT
003 003 323         OUT     /OUTPUT MODE CONTROL BYTE TO
003 004 203         CNTRL   /PPI CONTROL REGISTER
003 005 076         MVIA    /SET INTEA(PC4) USING BIT
003 006 011         INTEAS  /SET/RESET CONTROL BYTE
003 007 323         OUT
003 010 203         CNTRL
003 011 076         MVIA    /SET INTEB(PC2) USING BIT
003 012 005         INTEBS  /SET/RESET CONTROL BYTE
003 013 323         OUT
003 014 203         CNTRL
003 015 373         EI
                   /
                   /THIS IS THE BEGINNING OF THE
                   /INTERRUPT SERVICE ROUTINE.
                   /
                   *003 060
003 060 365 RESTRT, PUSHPSW /SAVE MICROCOMPUTER STATUS
003 061 345         PUSHH
003 062 325         PUSHD
003 063 305         PUSHB
003 064 333         IN      /INPUT MODE STATUS WORD FROM
003 065 202         PORTC   /PORT C
003 066 107         MOVBA   /SAVE MODE 1 STATUS WORD
003 067 346         ANI     /PORT B INTERRUPTING?
003 070 001         MASKB   /MASK BYTE FOR INTRB(D0)
003 071 302         JNZ     /YES! - JUMP TO SERVICE
003 072 200         PBSVC   /THE PORT B PERIPHERAL
003 073 003         0
003 074 170         MOVAB   /NO? - RESTORE STATUS WORD
003 075 346         ANI     /PORT A INTERRUPTING?
003 076 010         MASKA   /MASK BYTE FOR INTRA(D3)
003 077 302         JNZ     /YES! - JUMP TO SERVICE THE
003 100 300         PASVC   /PORT A PERIPHERAL
003 101 003         0
003 102 301         POPB    /NO, IGNORE INTERRUPT
003 103 321         POPD    /RESTORE MICROCOMPUTER STATUS
003 104 341         POPH
003 105 361         POPPSW
003 106 311         RET     /AND RETURN
```

Fig. 6-12. Program 6-1.

with the polled-interrupt service routine. In writing the program the author began by writing the PPI initialization code and polled-interrupt service routine in mnemonics adding comments to show the program structure. Variables such as the mode control byte, bit set bytes, mask bytes, and PPI addresses were given symbolic names. Now read the program listing in mnemonics and watch for these points.

Program 6-1 (Fig. 6-12)

An important feature of this program is the determination of the values for the variables. The addresses of the PPI control register and port C are a function of the way in which the PPI is wired to the microcomputer address lines, and so for this example we have used 203 and 202, respectively. The remaining variables were determined as follows:

(a) *MODE.* This is the mode control byte which is required to configure port A for mode 1 input operation, port B for mode 1 output operation, and port C upper bits PC6 and PC7 for output. From Fig. 2-2A the required byte is 10110100 or 264.

(b) *INTEAS, INTEBS.* These are the bit-set/reset control bytes required to set the $INTE_A$ and $INTE_B$, interrupt enable flags, of ports A and B, respectively. Referring to the mode 1 status word in Fig. 6-9, it will be seen that the interrupt enable flag for port A ($INTE_A$) is represented by different port C bits, depending upon whether port A is used for input or output. In this example port A is used for input (*cf* Fig. 6-8) and so port C bit D4 must be set to logic 1 using the PPI port C bit-set/reset feature. Referring to Fig. 2-2B the required bit-set/reset control byte is 00001001 or 011. The port B interrupt enable flip-flop is controlled by setting and resetting port C bit D2 (*cf* Fig. 6-9). The bit-set/reset control byte (from Fig. 2-2B) required to set PC2 is 00000101 = 005.

(c) *MASKA, MASKB.* These are the mask bytes that are required to mask out all of the mode 1 status word bits except those giving the status of the port A and port B interrupt request flags $INTR_A$ and $INTR_B$, respectively. For port A input, $INTR_A$ is represented by bit D3 of the mode 1 status word (Fig. 6-9) and hence MASKA is 00001000 or 010. $INTR_B$

is represented by bit D0 of the mode 1 status word and so is 00000001 or 001.

(d) *PASVC and PBSVC.* These represent the low address bytes for the port A and B service routines, respectively, and have been arbitrarily set in this program to 300 and 200, respectively.

In conclusion this example has been presented to illustrate the design approach to using a PPI for mode 1 handshaking I/O. For the hardware the major points to be evaluated include:

- Port and control line allocation.
- Vector interrupt, polled interrupt, or continuous software polling.
- Peripheral priority.
- If vector interrupt or polled interrupt, then the RST instructions to be jammed onto the data bus during an interrupt.

For software the major considerations include:

- Writing the PPI initialization code.
- For vector interrupt, writing and properly locating in memory the peripheral service routines.
- For polled interrupt, writing and properly locating in memory the software to determine which peripheral is interrupting.

The necessary variables which must be determined are:

- The mode control byte.
- The bit-set/reset control bytes required to set $INTE_A$ and/or $INTE_B$.
- The masking bytes required to determine the status of $INTR_A$ and/or $INTR_B$.
- The PPI addresses for ports A through C and for the control register.

6-5. SUMMARY OF EXPERIMENTS 6-1 THROUGH 6-5

Experiment	Description
6-1	The purpose of this experiment is to demonstrate the *mode 1 output* operation of the 8255 using the technique of *continuous software polling*. The use

of handshaking between the microcomputer and a pulser is also illustrated.

6-2   The purpose of this experiment is to demonstrate the *mode 1 input* operation of the 8255 using the technique of *continuous software polling.*

6-3   This experiment illustrates the *mode 1 operation* of the 8255 for *combined input and output* by *continuous software polling.*

6-4   This experiment illustrates the mode 1 *polled-interrupt* operation of the 8255.

6-5   The purpose of this experiment is to illustrate the mode 1 *vectored-interrupt* operation of the PPI.

EXPERIMENT 6-1
MODE 1 OUTPUT OPERATION OF THE PPI

Purpose

The purpose of this experiment is to demonstrate the *mode 1 output operation* of the 8255 integrated-circuit chip. The use of handshaking between the microcomputer and pulser will also be illustrated.

Step 1

Fig. 6-15 shows the Intel Corporation information on the mode 1 operation of ports A and B as output ports.

In this experiment we shall employ mode control word 240, which assigns port A as a mode 1 output port. Bit D3 in the control word is logic 0, which means that PC4 and PC5 have been configured as outputs.

Step 2

Connect the circuit shown in the schematic diagram (Fig. 6-14). Connect PC6 ($\overline{ACK}_A$) to the "1" output of the pulser. This is the pulser's output that is normally at logic 1.

Step 3

Load the program into memory. Explain what the control words at LO memory addresses 001 and 002 mean. At which addresses in the program are they loaded into the control register of the 8255 chip?

Schematic Diagram of Circuit (Fig. 6-13)

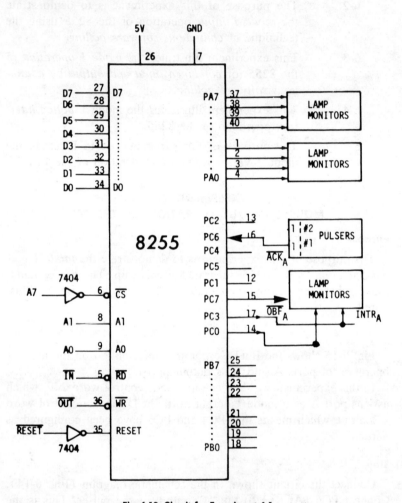

Fig. 6-13. Circuit for Experiment 6-1.

The control byte at LO memory address 001 is the mode control byte and this is loaded into the control register of the PPI with instructions commencing at LO memory address 003. The control byte at LO memory address 002 is the bit-set/reset control byte that is output to the control register with instructions commencing at LO memory address 010.

Program (Fig. 6-14)

```
            /
            /PPI MODE ONE OUTPUT OPERATION
            /
            DB CNTRL 203
            DB DATA1 200
            DB DATA3 202
            *003 000
003 000 001         LXIB      /LOAD PAIR B WITH THE FOLLOWING BYTES
003 001 240         240       /PPI MODE CONTROL WORD
003 002 015         015       /PPI BIT SET/RESET CONTROL WORD
003 003 171         MOVAC     /MOVE MODE CONTROL WORD TO ACCUMULATOR
003 004 323         OUT       /OUTPUT ACCUMULATOR CONTENTS TO THE
003 005 203         CNTRL     /PPI CONTROL REGISTER
003 006 026         MVID      /LOAD REGISTER D WITH 377
003 007 377         377
003 010 170         MOVAB     /LOAD A WITH PPI BIT SET/RESET CONTROL
003 011 323         OUT       /OUTPUT IT TO THE
003 012 203         CNTRL     /PPI CONTROL REGISTER
003 013 172   LOOP, MOVAD     /ZERO THE ACCUMULATOR
003 014 323         OUT       /OUTPUT ACCUMULATOR CONTENTS TO
003 015 200         DATA1     /PORT A
003 016 024         INRD      /INCREMENT REGISTER D CONTENTS BY 1
003 017 172         MOVAD
003 020 323         OUT       /DISPLAY NEXT OUTPUT BYTE
003 021 001         001       /AT PORT #1
003 022 333   WAIT, IN        /INPUT THE STATUS OF THE 8255, I.E.,
003 023 202         DATA3     /THE CONTENTS OF PORT C
003 024 323         OUT       /DISPLAY PPI STATUS AT
003 025 000         000       /PORT #0
003 026 346         ANI       /AND THE FOLLOWING MASK BYTE WITH
003 027 010         010       /THE ACCUMULATOR CONTENTS. THIS MASKS
                              /ALL BITS EXCEPT BIT 3 (INTRA)
003 030 312         JZ        /INTRA=1; NO:-TRY AGAIN
003 031 022         WAIT
003 032 003         0
003 033 303         JMP       /YES, PPI OUTPUT BUFFER EMPTY SO JUMP TO
003 034 013         LOOP      /JUMP TO OUTPUT ANOTHER BYTE
003 035 003         0
```

Fig. 6-14. Program for Experiment 6-1.

Step 4

Execute the program. Press and release the pulser several times. What do you observe at output port A?

We observed that the output at port A was incremented by one each time the pulser was pressed and released. While the pulser was pressed in [sending PC6 ($\overline{ACK}_A$) to logic 0], PC7 ($\overline{OBF}_A$) went to logic 0. Output PC3 (INTR$_A$) remained at logic 0, according to our visual indication. However, when we employed the simple counting circuit shown in Fig. 6-16, we observed one count each time that

Output Control Signal Definition

$\overline{OBF}$ (Output Buffer Full F/F)

The $\overline{OBF}$ output will go "low" to indicate that the CPU has written data out to the specified port. The OBF F/F will be set by the rising edge of the WR input and reset by the falling edge of the $\overline{ACK}$ input signal.

$\overline{ACK}$ (Acknowledge Input)

A "low" on this input informs the 825 that the data from Port A or Port B has been accepted. In essence, a response from the peripheral device indicating that it has received the data output by the CPU.

INTR (Interrupt Request)

A "high" on this output can be used to interrupt the CPU when an output device has accepted data transmitted by the CPU. INTR is set by the rising edge of $\overline{ACK}$ if $\overline{OBF}$ is a "one" and INTE is a "one". It is reset by the falling edge of $\overline{WR}$.

INTE A

Controlled by bit set/reset of PC_6.

INTE B

Controlled by bit set/reset of PC_2.

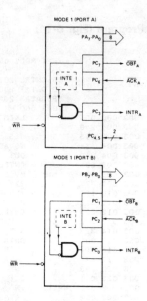

Fig. 6-15. Mode 1 operation of ports A and B as output ports.

the pulser was pressed and released. This means that the PC3 connection generated a single pulse each time the pulser was pressed and released.

Step 5

Carefully examine the program steps. Can you identify the program steps which cause the microcomputer to "loop" once the program is executed. If you have trouble answering this question, study the mode 1 output timing diagram given in Fig. 6-17. Look at the relationship between $\overline{ACK}_A$ (PC6) and $INTR_A$ (PC3).

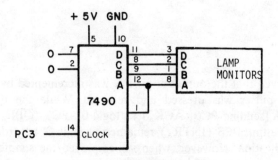

Fig. 6-16. Simple counting circuit.

When the program is first started, the PPI is initialized (LO addresses 000 through 012) for mode 1 operation with port A configured for output. The microcomputer then transfers data to port A (LO addresses 013 through 015). This sets the Output Buffer Full (OBF) flag to logic 0 to indicate that data has been transferred to port A. The program then waits in the WAIT loop (LO addresses

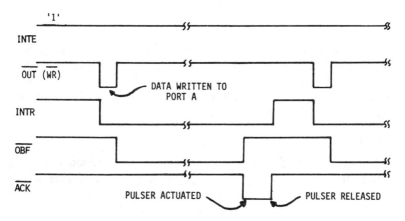

Fig. 6-17. Mode 1 output timing.

022 through 032) until it detects the presence of the INTR$_A$ flag which is checked in software. The INTR$_A$ signal is set to logic 1 when you acknowledge ($\overline{ACK}_A$) that you (the peripheral) have received the data. Once you acknowledge receipt of the data a new (incremented) data byte is output and the process is repeated.

What happens when you press the pulser ($\overline{ACK}_A = 0$) and hold it in? Use Fig. 6-17 timing diagrams to help you with your answer.

The answer is that the $\overline{ACK}_A$ input to the PPI goes to logic 0 and the $\overline{OBF}_A$ output goes to logic 1. As long as the pulser remains pressed in, nothing else happens.

Step 6

Now explain what occurs when you release the pulser. (*Hint:* What happens on the rising edge of $\overline{ACK}_A$ if both INTE$_A$ and $\overline{OBF}_A$ are at logic 1?) Make certain that you explain what happens to the output at port A. Please give a detailed answer.

When you release the $\overline{ACK}_A$ pulser ($\overline{ACK}_A = 1$), you have acknowledged receipt of the data that was previously output to port A by the 8080 and displayed on the lamp monitors. A new data byte is then output. This is indicated by the Output Buffer Full flag ($\overline{OBF}_A$) going to a logic 0 again.

Step 7

Change the bit-set/reset control word at LO memory address 002 to 014. When this byte is output to the control register it will cause the internal PPI flip-flop, $INTE_A$, to be reset to logic 0. Will this have an effect on the operation of the interface?

Yes. "It turns off" the port A interrupts so that $INTR_A$ cannot be set to logic 1.

Step 8

With the change in your software (made in Step 7), execute the program. Repeatedly press and release the pulser. Is *any* data transferred to port A?

Yes, data is transferred, but only the first byte, 377.

Explain why the program change had such an effect. You may find the timing diagram of Fig. 6-18 useful in your explanation. Note that the output, $INTR_A$, never goes to logic 1. You can confirm this behavior with the aid of the 7490 counter circuit given in Step 4. With the internal interrupt enable ($INTE_A$) turned off, the acknowledge signal is not gated through to PC3, the $INTR_A$ output.

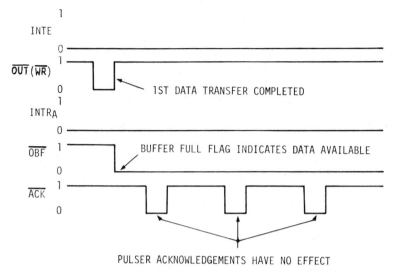

INTE

$\overline{OUT}$ ($\overline{WR}$)

1ST DATA TRANSFER COMPLETED

INTR$_A$

$\overline{OBF}$ BUFFER FULL FLAG INDICATES DATA AVAILABLE

$\overline{ACK}$

PULSER ACKNOWLEDGEMENTS HAVE NO EFFECT

Fig. 6-18. Timing diagram for program change.

Questions

1. A key step in the program is the IN instruction given at LO memory address 022. If you have successfully answered the questions given in the preceding steps, then you already understand why we input the status of the 8255 chip into the accumulator. In the space below, explain why.

2. The status word for mode 1 operation when either port A or port B is an output port is given by Intel as in Fig. 6-19.
   (a) What is the significance of bits D3, D6, and D7?

   (b) What is the significance of mask byte 010 at LO memory address 027? Why do we use it rather than either 300 or 100?

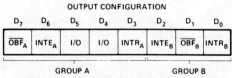

OUTPUT CONFIGURATION

D_7	D_6	D_5	D_4	D_3	D_2	D_1	D_0
$\overline{OBF}_A$	$INTE_A$	I/O	I/O	$INTR_A$	$INTE_B$	$\overline{OBF}_B$	$INTR_B$

GROUP A   GROUP B

Fig. 6-19. Status word for mode 1 operation with port A or port B as an output port.

3. What changes must be made to the program given in this experiment to permit it to be used for the mode 1 operation of output port B? *Hint:* The changes need to be made at the following LO memory address.

LO Memory Address	Port A Output	Port B Output
001	240	
002	015	
015	200	
027	010	

4. Complete the schematic diagram given in Fig. 6-20 for the mode 1 output operation of port B. We want eight lamp monitors at port B, a pulser input to the appropriate input at port C, and the $\overline{OBF}_B$ and $INTR_B$ outputs connected to a pair of lamp monitors.

EXPERIMENT 6-2
MODE 1 INPUT OPERATION OF THE PPI

Purpose

The purpose of this experiment is to demonstrate the *mode 1 input operation* of the 8255 integrated-circuit chip. The use of handshaking is again illustrated.

Schematic Diagram of Circuit (Fig. 6-21)

NOTE: If you have just completed Experiment 6-1, you will have other hardware connected to your interface. This is not shown in this diagram for the sake of clarity.

Step 1

The author recommends that you use the 7490 decade counter circuit in Fig. 6-23 to follow and monitor the behavior of the program in Fig. 6-22 and 8255 circuit. Connect output PC0 ($INTR_B$) to the 7490 decade counter.

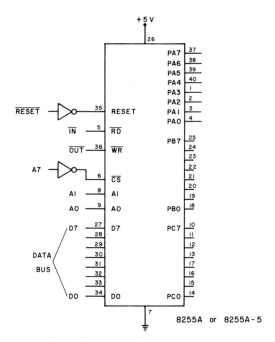

Fig. 6-20. Schematic diagram to be completed.

Step 2

Shown in Fig. 6-24 are the Intel Corporation specifications of the mode 1 operation of ports A and B as *input* ports.

In this experiment, you will use mode control word 246 to configure port B as an input port. Bit D3 is at logic 0, which means that PC6 and PC7 are configured for output operation. The port C status word for mode 1 operation when either port A or port B is an input port is given by Intel as shown in Fig. 6-25. Bit D0 ($INTR_B$) of this port C status word is set to logic 1 when data is available at port B for input to the microcomputer (assuming that INTE = 1). Bit D0 is checked in the program and data is input from port B only when D0 ($INTR_B$) goes to logic 1.

Step 3

Wire the circuit shown in the schematic diagram (Fig. 6-21). Wire port C bit PC2 ($\overline{STB}_B$) to the 1 output on the pulser.

Step 4

Load the program into memory and execute the program.

149

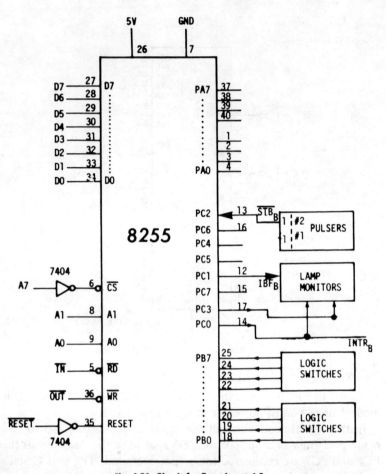

Fig. 6-21. Circuit for Experiment 6-2.

Step 5

Set the logic switches to 01001001 and press and release the pulser. What do you observe at port 0? What change do you observe on the 7490 decade counter?

We observed an output of 111 at the port 0 LED display, as expected. The 7490 counter detected a single count. The lamp monitor connected to PC1 (IBF$_B$) remained lit for as long as the pulser was pressed.

Program (Fig. 6-22)

```
        /
        /PPI MODE 1 INPUT PROGRAM
        /
        DB CNTRL 203
        DB DATA3 202
        DB DATA2 201
        *003 000
003 000 001        LXIB    /LOAD REGISTER PAIR B WITH
003 001 246        246     /C REGISTER: MODE CONTROL WORD
003 002 005        005     /B REGISTER: BIT SET CONTROL WORD
003 003 171        MOVAC   /LOAD THE ACCUMULATOR WITH THE
                           /MODE CONTROL WORD
003 004 323        OUT     /OUTPUT IT TO THE
003 005 203        CNTRL   /CONTROL REGISTER
003 006 170        MOVAB   /LOAD THE ACCUMULATOR WITH THE
                           /BIT SET/RESET CONTROL WORD
003 007 323        OUT     /OUTPUT IT TO THE
003 010 203        CNTRL   /CONTROL REGISTER
003 011 333  WAIT, IN      /INPUT THE 8255 STATUS BYTE FROM
003 012 202        DATA3   /PORT C
003 013 323        OUT     /OUTPUT PORT C STATUS BYTE FOR DISPLAY
003 014 000        000
003 015 346        ANI     /MASK BIT D0:-INTRB
003 016 001        001
003 017 312        JZ      /INTRB ="0"?
003 020 011        WAIT    /YES, LOOP TO WAIT FOR DATA TO BE
003 021 003        0       /LOADED INTO THE PPI PORT B INPUT BUFFER
003 022 333        IN      /INTRB ="1", SO INPUT THE DATA AT
003 023 201        DATA2   /PORT B
003 024 323        OUT     /OUTPUT DATA
003 025 000        000     /DEVICE CODE OF PORT 0
003 026 303        JMP     /JUMP TO LOOK FOR NEW DATA
003 027 011        WAIT
003 030 003        0
```

Fig. 6-22. Program for Experiment 6-2.

Step 6

Change the logic switch setting and press and release the pulser after each change. In each case you should observe that the data at the logic switches appears at port 0.

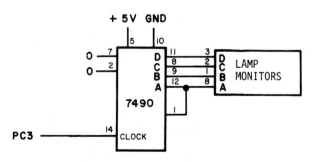

Fig. 6-23. Decade counter circuit.

Input Control Signal Definition

$\overline{\text{STB}}$ (Strobe Input)

A "low" on this input loads data into the input latch.

IBF (Input Buffer Full F/F)

A "high" on this output indicates that the data has been loaded into the input latch; in essence, an acknowledgement. IBF is set by the falling edge of the STB input and is reset by the rising edge of the RD input.

INTR (Interrupt Request)

A "high" on this output can be used to interrupt the CPU when an input device is requesting service. INTR is set by the rising edge of STB if IBF is a "one" and INTE is a "one". It is reset by the falling edge of $\overline{\text{RD}}$. This procedure allows an input device to request service from the CPU by simply strobing its data into the port.

 INTE A

Controlled by bit set/reset of PC_4.

 INTE B

Controlled by bit set/reset of PC_2.

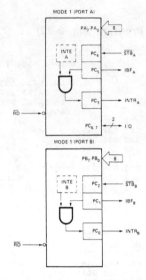

Courtesy Intel Corp.

Fig. 6-24. Mode 1 operation of ports A and B as input ports.

Step 7

 Among what program steps does the program loop once it has been started? Why?

 The program loops between addresses 003 011 and 003 017. This is the loop in which the INTR_B flag is tested. The program will only leave this loop when the pulser has been pressed and released and INTR_B has been set to logic 1.

 Change the switch settings to a new 8-bit pattern. Press the pulser and keep it pressed. Does any action take place when it is pressed in?

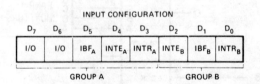

INPUT CONFIGURATION

D_7	D_6	D_5	D_4	D_3	D_2	D_1	D_0
I/O	I/O	IBF_A	$INTE_A$	$INTR_A$	$INTE_B$	IBF_B	$INTR_B$

GROUP A   GROUP B

Fig. 6-25. Port C status word for mode 1 operation when either port A or port B is an input port.

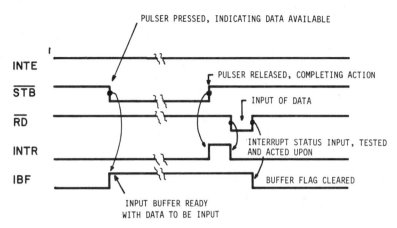

Fig. 6-26. Action of pressing and releasing pulser.

No action takes place until the pulser is released. This is shown clearly in Fig. 6-26.

Step 8

What now happens when you release the pulser? You leave the loop, obviously. What else occurs? Use the timing diagram of Fig. 6-26 to aid in your explanation.

Action takes place in that the new 8-bit pattern is transferred to the output port lamp monitors.

Step 9

Change the byte at LO memory address 002 to 004. This control byte causes the internal flip-flop output, $INTE_B$, to be reset to logic 0.

Again run the program. Repeatedly press and release the pulser as you change the settings of the logic switches. Do you observe any changes at output port 0?

We observed no changes.

Explain why the program change at memory address 003 002 had such an effect. (*Hint:* The Intel literature states that "INTR is set by the rising edge of $\overline{STB}$ if IBF is a logic 1 and INTE is a logic 1.")

When $INTE_B$ is a logic 0, the $INTR_B$ flag is never set to logic 1 by $\overline{STB}_B$ and so there is no way for the program to exit from the WAIT loop.

Questions

1. Complete the schematic diagram given in Fig. 6-27 for the mode 1 operation of input port A. You will need eight logic switches at

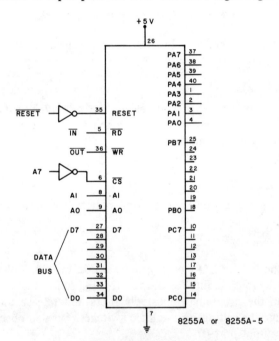

Fig. 6-27. Schematic diagram to be completed.

port A, a pulser to strobe the $\overline{STB}_A$ input, and two lamp monitors that are connected to IBF_A and $INTR_A$.

2. List below the changes that must be made to the program given in this experiment to permit port A to be used for mode 1 input operation.

LO Memory Address	Port A Input	Port B Input
001		206
002		005
016		001
023		201

NOTE:Retain the circuit you wired in this experiment for the following experiment.

EXPERIMENT 6-3
COMBINED MODE 1 INPUT AND OUTPUT
OPERATION OF THE PPI

Purpose

The purpose of this experiment is to demonstrate the mode 1 operation of the 8255 for combined input and output using port B for input and port A for output. The concept of *handshaking* is also illustrated. This experiment is a synthesis of the procedures in Experiments 6-1 and 6-2. If you feel you have grasped the procedures required for mode 1 I/O operation of the 8255, you may want to write and test a program that will input data (from logic switches) at port B and output this data (to lamp monitors) at port A. Our program is listed in Fig. 6-28.

Step 1

Wire the circuit shown in Fig. 6-29. You will also require a bus monitor as shown in Fig. 6-30.

Step 2

Load the program into memory.

Step 3

Start the program. Set the logic switches to 1111 1111. Is the data transferred to the lamp monitors? Why?

No, data was not transferred to the port B lamp monitors since the PPI has not flagged the 8080 that its port B input buffer is full.

Program (Fig. 6-28)

```
                    /
                    /THIS PROGRAM INPUTS DATA FROM PORT B
                    /AND OUTPUTS IT TO PORT A
                    /
                    DB PC2SET 005
                    DB PORTA 200
                    DB PORTB 201
                    DB PORTC 202
                    DB CNTRL 203
                    *003 000
003 000 001              LXIB        /LOAD REGISTER PAIR B WITH:
003 001 246              246         /PPI MODE CONTROL WORD
003 002 015              015         /PPI BIT-SET CONTROL WORD(SETS INTEA)
003 003 026              MVID        /LOAD REGISTER D WITH:
003 004 005              PC2SET      /PPI BIT-SET/RESET WORD (SETS INTEB)
003 005 171              MOVAC       /LOAD A WITH MODE CONTROL BYTE
003 006 323              OUT         /OUTPUT IT TO THE
003 007 203              CNTRL       /PPI'S CONTROL REGISTER
003 010 170              MOVAB       /LOAD A WITH PC6SET
003 011 323              OUT         /OUTPUT IT TO THE
003 012 203              CNTRL       /PPI'S CONTROL REGISTER
003 013 172              MOVAD       /LOAD A WITH PC2SET
003 014 323              OUT         /OUTPUT IT TO THE
003 015 203              CNTRL       /PPI'S CONTROL REGISTER
003 016 333       WAITB,  IN          /INPUT PPI'S STATUS FROM PORT C
003 017 202              PORTC
003 020 346              ANI         /MASK OUT ALL BITS
003 021 001              001         /EXCEPT BIT D0(INTRB)
003 022 323              OUT         /OUTPUT RESULT TO PORT 0
003 023 000              000
003 024 312              JZ          /INTRB="0",SO TRY AGAIN
003 025 016              WAITB
003 026 003              0

003 027 333              IN          /INTRB ="1", SO INPUT DATA
003 030 201              PORTB       /FROM PORT B
003 031 323              OUT         /OUTPUT DATA BYTE TO:
003 032 200              PORTA       /PORT A
003 033 333       WAITA,  IN          /INPUT PPI STATUS WORD FROM
003 034 202              PORTC       /PORT C
003 035 346              ANI         /MASK OUT ALL BITS EXCEPT
003 036 010              010                      /BIT D3(INTRA)
003 037 312              JZ          /INTRA="0", SO TRY AGAIN
003 040 033              WAITA
003 041 003              0
003 042 303              JMP         /INTRA ="1". DATA ACCEPTED AT
003 043 016              WAITB       /PORT A SO JUMP TO INPUT
003 044 003              0           /A NEW BYTE FROM PORT B
```

Fig. 6-28. Program for Experiment 6-3.

Step 4

Press and release pulser #1. This is the port B data strobe signal $\overline{STB}_B$. Does this cause the data to be transferred? Why?

Schematic Diagram of Circuit (Fig. 6-29)

NOTE: The schematic diagram represents the circuitry that was connected and used in Experiments 6-1 and 6-2. If all your wiring is intact, go on to examine the program that is provided or to write your own program.

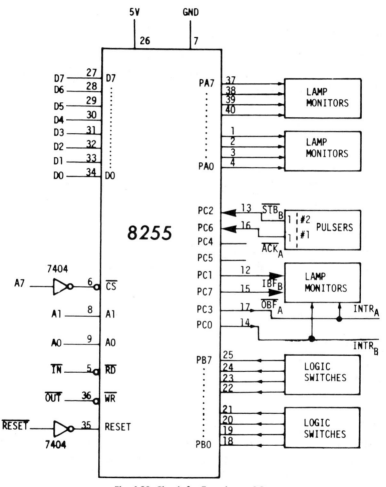

Fig. 6-29. Circuit for Experiment 6-3.

Yes. This action strobes data into the port B input buffer, causing the port B input buffer full flag to go to logic 1. The program detects this, inputs the data at port B, and then outputs it to port A.

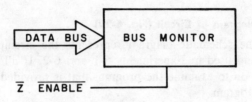

Fig. 6-30. Bus monitor arrangement.

Step 5

Change the logic switch setting to 0000 0000. Again press and release pulser #1. Is this data transferred? Why? If you are in doubt, examine the program at WAITA.

No, data was not transferred since the program is now waiting for the output device (lamp monitors) to acknowledge its receipt of the data byte.

Step 6

Press and release pulser #2, the acknowledge control signal for port A ($\overline{ACK_A}$). What is now observed at port A?

You should observe that the 0s are finally transferred. Remember that you just acknowledged receipt of the 1s, so press and release pulser #2 again to indicate that the lamp monitors have received the 0s.

Step 7

Repeatedly change the switch settings and press and release pulser #2 and pulser #1. Is the switch data transferred now?

Yes, after a complete cycle of pulser #1 and pulser #2 activations have been completed.

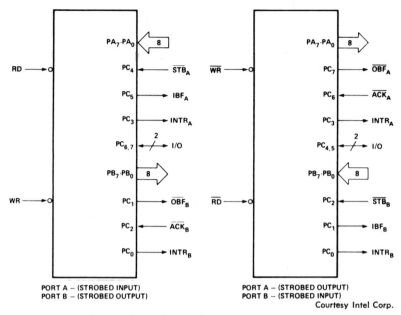

PORT A – (STROBED INPUT)
PORT B – (STROBED OUTPUT)

PORT A – (STROBED OUTPUT)
PORT B – (STROBED INPUT)

Courtesy Intel Corp.

Fig. 6-31. Two mode 1 combinations for ports A and B.

Step 8

Shown in this step are block diagrams (Fig. 6-31) for the use of two of the four possible mode 1 combinations for ports A and B. Which of these block diagrams applies to this experiment? Provide evidence with your answer.

The diagram on the right-hand side represents the mode 1 configuration that has been implemented in this experiment since port B is used for input (from our logic switches) and port A is used for output (to the lamp monitors).

Step 9

Write the mode 1 status word format for this particular experiment.

The required mode 1 status word can be constructed from Fig. 6-9, remembering that group B is configured for input and group A for output.

The program given in this experiment employs two of the 8 bits for the mode 1 status word. Which bits are used? Why?

In loop, WAITB, of the program we have monitored bit D0 ($INTR_B$) of the mode 1 status word. This signal goes high when data has been loaded into the port B input buffer and is ready for input to the 8080A. In loop, WAITA, we have monitored bit D3 ($INTR_A$) of the mode 1 status word since this signal goes to logic 1 when the output peripheral at port A has acknowledged receipt of the data sent to port A. We do this in this experiment by pressing and releasing pulser #2 ($\overline{ACK_A}$).

Step 10

A set of timing diagrams that depict the operation of this program are shown in Fig. 6-32.

Reset your microcomputer, run the program and switch to single-step operation. $\overline{STB_B}$ is generated by pulser #1 and $\overline{ACK_A}$ is generated to pulser #2. Begin single-stepping through your program while monitoring IBF_B, $INTR_B$, $\overline{OBF_A}$, and $\overline{ACK_A}$. Through what steps is the program looping?

The program is in the loop, WAITB between memory locations 003 016 and 003 026, waiting for $INTR_B$ to go high. This situation is depicted on the far left of the timing diagram. Step through the loop and stop at the third machine cycle, the input machine cycle,

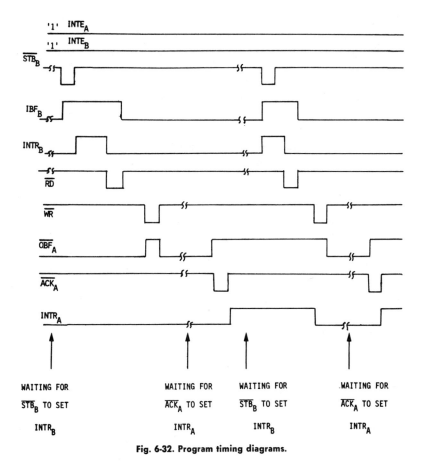

Fig. 6-32. Program timing diagrams.

of the input instruction. Now press and release pulser #1, the $\overline{STB}_B$ signal and continue single-stepping. Note below what you observe.

We observed:

(a) IBF$_B$ went high when the pulser was pressed.

(b) INTR$_B$ went to logic 1 when the pulser was released. Both these actions were observed in the mode 1 status word and on the lamp monitors.

(c) Data from the logic switches was input during the third machine cycle of the IN instruction at memory location 003 030. INTR$_B$ was reset here.

(d) The IBF$_B$ flag was reset during the *next* machine cycle.

(e) The program, after outputting the byte to port A, then looped in the WAITA loop (memory locations 003 033 through 003 041) waiting for INTR$_A$ to go high.

Now stop in the third machine cycle of the input instruction at location 003 034. You are observing the mode 1 status word on the bus monitor. Press and release pulser #2. What changes do you observe to the mode 1 status word and on the lamp monitors at port C?

When the pulser was pressed, $\overline{OBF}_A$ went to logic 1. When the pulser was released, INTR$_A$ went to logic 1.

Continue single-stepping. Where does the program go? Why?

The program enters the loop, WAITB, after exiting WAITA, to input a byte from port B.

Repeat the entire procedure of Step 10 again and confirm the remainder of the timing diagram.

Step 11

We have used the single-step procedure here to illustrate the timing operation of the PPI for mode 1 input and output operation. From Step 10, can you suggest an important application of the single-step facility?

The single-step facility is very useful in debugging an interface and its associated software driver. By single-stepping through the software driver and stopping at the third machine cycle of input and output instructions, the bytes that are input from the interface as status and data can be checked for any possible errors. Similarly, the data bytes that are output to the interface can be checked.

NOTE: Retain your circuit for the following experiment.

EXPERIMENT 6-4
MODE 1 POLLED-INTERRUPT PPI OPERATION

Purpose

The purpose of this experiment is to illustrate the *mode 1 polled-interrupt operation* of the 8255.

Step 1

Wire the circuits shown in Fig. 6-35. Note that all the wiring connections to the PPI are identical with those used in Experiment 6-3 except for the reconnection of the INTR$_A$ and INTR$_B$ lines. Hence, if you have completed this experiment, only the INTR$_A$ and INTR$_B$ connections need be altered. Make sure that pins PC2 ($\overline{STB}_B$) and PC6 ($\overline{ACK}_A$) of the PPI are connected to the logic 1 outputs of the two pulsers.

Step 2

Load the program into the read/write memory of the micro-computer.

Step 3

Study the program listing. You will see that there are four major blocks of instructions of varying lengths. In the space below list the starting memory locations for each of these blocks and briefly describe their functions.

Program (Fig. 6-33)

```
003 127 015   LOOP2,   DCRC
003 130 302            JNZ
003 131 127            LOOP2
003 132 003            0
003 133 303            JMP
003 134 123            LOOP1
003 135 003            0
          /      .
          /      .
          /      .
          /      .
          *003 150
003 150 365   SEARCH,  PUSHPSW  /COMMENCE SEARCH FOR SOURCE
                                /OF INTERRUPT
003 151 305            PUSHB
003 152 333            IN       /INPUT MODE 1 STATUS WORD
003 153 202            PORTC
003 154 107            MOVBA    /SAVE IT
003 155 346            ANI      /MASK BIT D3 (INTRA)
003 156 010            010      /PORT A INTRRUPTING?
003 157 302            JNZ      /YES! -JUMP TO PORT A
003 160 250            PASVCE   /SERVICE ROUTINE
003 161 003            0
003 162 170            MOVAB    /NO, RESTORE MODE 1 STATUS WORD
003 163 346            ANI      /MASK BIT D0 =INTRB
003 164 001            001      /PORT B INTERRUPTING?
003 165 302            JNZ      /YES! -JUMP TO PORT B
003 166 210            PBSVCE   /SERVICE ROUTINE
003 167 003            0
003 170 301            POPB     /NO? -IGNORE INTERRUPT
003 171 361            POPPSW
003 172 311            RET
          /      .
          /      .
          /      .
          /      .
          *003 210
003 210 333   PBSVCE,  IN       /INPUT DATA FROM PORT B
003 211 201            PORTB
003 212 323            OUT      /OUTPUT IT TO PORT 0
003 213 000            000          .
003 214 127            MOVDA
003 215 303            JMP      /JUMP TO PORT A
003 216 250            PASVCE   /SERVICE ROUTINE
003 217 003            0
          /      .
          /      .
          /      .
          /      .
          *003 250
003 250 024   PASVCE,  INRD     /INCREMENT D
003 251 172            MOVAD    /MOVE CONTENTS OF D TO ACCUMULATOR
003 252 323            OUT      /OUTPUT CONTENTS OF D TO
003 253 200            PORTA    /PORT A
003 254 301            POPB     /RESTORE MICROCOMPUTER STATUS
```

Fig. 6-33. Program for

Schematic Diagram of Circuit (Fig. 6-35)

The major functional blocks of instructions commence at LO memory addresses 100, 150, 210, and 250. The first block is the PPI initialization code and wait loop. The second block is concerned with polling the PPI to determine the source of the interrupt. Blocks three and four are the port B and port A service routines respectively. The port B service subroutine inputs the logic switch data from port

```
003 255 361              POPPSW
003 256 373              EI       /ENABLE INTERRUPTS
003 257 311              RET
                    DB MODE 246
                    DB PORTA 200
                    DB PORTB 201
                    DB PORTC 202
                    DB CNTRL 203
                    DB PC6SET 015
                    DB PC2SET 005
                    *003 050
003 050 303              JMP      /PPI REQUIRES SERVICE
003 051 150              SEARCH   /JUMP TO SEARCH FOR
003 052 003              0        /SOURCE OF INTERRUPT
                    /      .
                    /      .
                    /      .
                    /      .
                    /      .
                    *003 100
003 100 061  START,  LXISP     /BEGIN PPI INITIALIZATION FOR
003 101 377          377       /MODE 1, POLLED INTERRUPT
003 102 003          003       /OPERATION
003 103 076          MVIA      /LOAD MODE 1 CONTROL WORD
003 104 246          MODE      /PORT A: OUTPUT; PORT B: INPUT
003 105 323          OUT
003 106 203          CNTRL
003 107 076          MVIA      /SET PPI BIT D6 (INTEA)
003 110 015          PC6SET
003 111 323          OUT
003 112 203          CNTRL
003 113 076          MVIA      /SET PPI BIT D2 (INTEB)
003 114 005          PC2SET
003 115 323          OUT
003 116 203          CNTRL
003 117 373          EI        /ENABLE THE 8080A FOR INTERRUPTS
003 120 001  WAIT,   LXIB      /BEGIN EXECUTION OF A
003 121 377          377       /WAIT LOOP
003 122 377          377
003 123 005  LOOP1,  DCRB
003 124 312          JZ
003 125 120          WAIT
003 126 003          0
```

Experiment 6-4.

Pin Configuration of Integrated-Circuit Chips (Fig. 6-34)

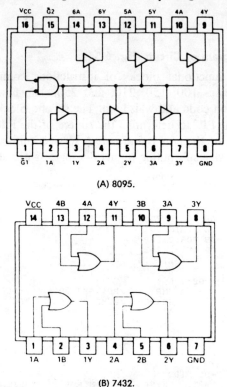

(A) 8095.

(B) 7432.

Fig. 6-34. Pin configurations of ICs.

B output to port 0, increments the data byte in register D, and outputs the results to port A. The port A service subroutine (PASVCE) increments the contents of register D and outputs the result to port A.

Two additional features should also be noted while studying the program. First, the device codes used to address port A, B, C, and the control register of the PPI are the same as those used in Experiments 6-1 to 6-3 since the wiring of the 8255 control lines $\overline{CS}$, A1, and A0 in this experiment is the same as that used in the earlier experiments. Second, since this is an interrupt experiment, the 8080A interrupt enable flag must be set before the microcomputer can be interrupted. The flag is set, using the EI instruction, *after* the PPI has been initialized to ensure that both $INTR_A$ and $INTR_B$ are both at logic 0.

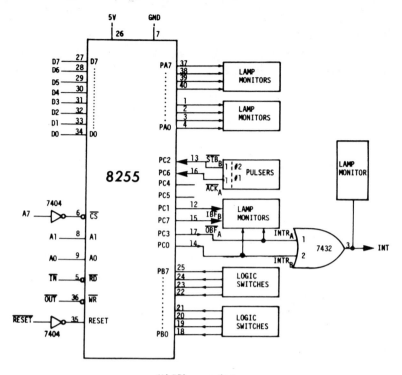

(A) PPI connections.

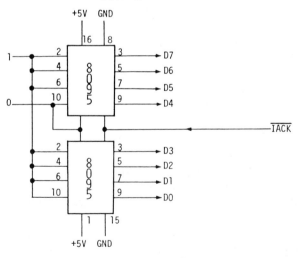

(B) 3-state buffer circuits.

Fig. 6-35. Circuits for Experiment 6-4.

Step 4

Execute the program commencing at address 003 100. Is the INT line at logic 1? If not, why not?

The interrupt line, INT, should be at logic 0 at this stage. A logic 1 would indicate that either $INTR_A$ or $INTR_B$ were at logic 1, hence requesting service for either port A or port B. This should only occur if the $\overline{STB}_B$ or $\overline{ACK}_A$ pulsers have been pressed.

Step 5

Set the logic switches to 000. Now press and release pulser #2 ($\overline{STB}_B$). Describe in the space below what you observe and relate this to the expected action of the program.

Pressing $\overline{STB}_B$ loads port B with the data byte set on the logic switches. When the pulser is released, $INTR_B$ and hence INT are set. This causes the microcomputer to be interrupted. A logic 0 on IACK, acknowledging the interrupt, causes the byte 357 or RST5 to be "jammed" into the instruction register. Program control is vectored via jumps at 000 050 and 003 050 to location 003 150 where through polling the PPI, it is determined that port B is interrupting. The port B service routine outputs the contents of port B firstly to port 0 and then, after incrementation, to port A. The data bytes 000 and 001 should be observed then at port 0 and port A respectively.

Step 6

Press and release the $\overline{ACK}_A$ pulser. Describe in the space below what you observed each time the pulser was pressed and released.

We observed that the contents of port A were incremented each time the pulser was pressed.

Step 7

Connect your bus monitor circuit to the data bus with its latch enable input wired to logic 0 so that the monitor is continuously enabled. Run your microcomputer in single-step mode. Press the $\overline{STB}_B$ pulser and note what happens to IBF_B. Release $\overline{STB}_B$ and note what happens to INT. Now commence single stepping through your program. After the microcomputer has completed its current instruction, you will observe the address of the instruction that will be executed on return from the interrupt being pushed on to the stack, the RST5 instruction on the data bus, and then program execution as described in Step 5. Write down the bytes that appear on the data bus and compare these with the program listing. Note the changes in $INTR_A$. The timing diagram is the same as that given in Fig. 6-32. Repeat the exercise when ACK_A is pressed. Once again take note of the changes in the PPI control and status lines. You will find Figs. 6-4 and 6-6 useful in understanding the operation of the circuit.

NOTE: Retain your program and circuit for the next experiment.

EXPERIMENT 6-5
MODE 1 VECTORED INTERRUPT OPERATION OF THE PPI

Purpose

The purpose of this experiment is to illustrate the *mode 1 vectored interrupt operation* of the PPI.

Schematic Diagram of Circuit (Fig. 6-36)

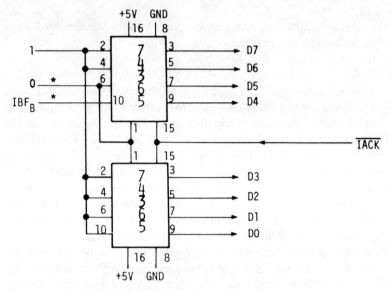

Fig. 6-36. Circuit for Experiment 6-5.

Program (Fig. 6-37)

```
                   DW  PASVCE 003 250
                   DW  PBSVCE 003 210
                   *003 010
003 010 365            PUSHPSW /STORE PROGRAM STATUS
003 011 305            PUSHB
003 012 303            JMP     /JUMP TO THE PORT A
003 013 250            PASVCE  /SERVICE SUBROUTINE
003 014 003            0
                /      .
                /      .
                /      .
                /      .
                *003 030
003 030 365            PUSHPSW /STORE PROGRAM STATUS
003 031 305            PUSHB
003 032 303            JMP     /JUMP TO THE PORT B
003 033 210            PBSVCE  /SERVICE SUBROUTINE
003 034 003            0
```

Fig. 6-37. Program for Experiment 6-5.

Step 1

The circuit for this experiment is the same as that used in the previous experiment except for two changes that have been made at the inputs of the 8095 (SN74365) three-state buffers and noted with an asterisk. Make the alterations shown in the schematic diagram of Fig. 6-36.

Step 2

The port A and B service routines and the PPI initialization code, which were loaded into memory in Experiment 6-4, will again be used in this experiment. Add the program instructions listed in Fig. 6-37 to memory. Note that the instructions at locations 003 050 through 003 052 and 003 150 through 003 172 will not be used in this experiment.

Step 3

The 8095 three-state buffer circuit shown in the schematic diagram is used to generate the two vector restart instructions that are jammed into the instruction register during a port A or port B interrupt. To generate these two vector restart instructions, the port B status line IBF_B is wired to the interrupt instruction buffer. By referring to Figs. 6-4 and 6-6, deduce the logic states of IBF_A *during an interrupt*. Complete Table 6-1 and hence deduce the restart instructions which are jammed into the instruction register during data input from port B and data output to port A.

Table 6-1. Restart Instruction Data

		RST Instruction	
	IBF_A	Binary	Octal
Port A Input Port B Output			

During port B input, IBF_B is at logic 1 and an RST 3(337) instruction is generated. During port A output, IBF_B is at logic 0 and an RST 1(317) instruction is generated.

Step 4

Execute the program commencing at location 003 100.

Step 5

Set the logic switches to 377. Press and release the $\overline{STB}_B$ pulser. Describe and explain what you observe.

We observed that the data byte 377 was output to the MMD-1 port 0 and the data byte 000 was output to the lamp monitors at port A. This is caused by microcomputer operation being vectored directly to the port B service routine whose operation was described in Step 5 of Experiment 6-4.

Step 6

Now press and release the $\overline{\text{ACK}}_A$ pulser several times. What do you observe?

We observed that the data byte at the port A lamp monitors was incremented by one each time the pulser was pressed and released.

Step 7

Switch the microcomputer to single-step operation. Press and release the $\overline{\text{ACK}}_A$ pulser. Now single-step through the microcomputer execution of the port A interrupt. Watch for the RST 1(317) instruction on the data bus using a bus monitor which is permanently enabled. Note the logic states of $\overline{\text{OBF}}_A$ and INT as you step through the program and compare these with those of Fig. 6-6. To keep track of program execution, you will find it helpful to write down in the space below the octal bytes you observe on the data bus and to compare these with the program.

The first few bytes which we observed were as follows:

***	Completion of current instruction
317	RST 1 instruction
003	HI address byte of program counter
127	LO address byte of program counter
303	Jump instruction in hex at 000 010
010	
003	
365	
.	
.	
.	
etc.	
.	
.	
.	

Mode 2 Operation: Bidirectional I/O

7-1. INTRODUCTION

With the introduction of the microcomputer the implementation of digital process control systems using a number of computers is becoming more popular. In this type of *distributed* computer control system a number of small computers—increasingly microcomputers —are dedicated to control small portions of the overall process. In a chemical process, for example, a microcomputer can be used to control a small portion of the process such as the pressure or temperature in, say, a distillation column. With microcomputers used in this way a larger computer with increased speed, memory, and disc storage (a minicomputer or a larger, more powerful microcomputer) is then used to *supervise* the operation of the overall process by monitoring and altering, by command as necessary, the operation of the dedicated microcomputer controllers. This leads naturally to the concept of a hierarchy of computer control. In the example given, the supervising computer was at a higher level than the dedicated microcomputers. Because of this, the supervising small computer or microcomputer is often referred to as the *master* while the lower-level, dedicated microcomputers are called *slaves*.

The master-slave concept is illustrated in Fig. 7-1, which also shows the role which the PPI can play in this situation. The essential requirement of a distributed computer control system is a two-way

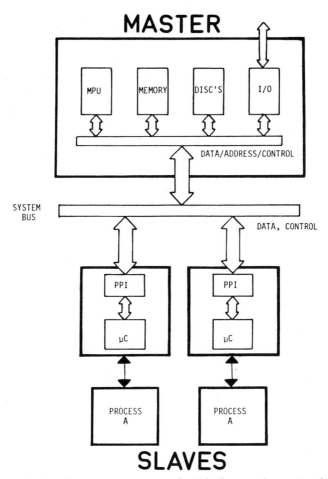

Fig. 7-1. A distributed computer process control which illustrates the way in which the PPI is used as an interface element between the bidirectional data busses of the master and slave MPUs.

transfer of data between master and slave microprocessor units (MPUs). This data may be in the form of *blocks of data* which are collected by the slave and transferred back to the master for processing; or it may be *set point data* which is passed by the master to the slave so that the slave can hold a process parameter (temperature, pressure, thickness, etc.) at a required value. Hence the slave MPU must be connected to the data and control bus of the master MPU.

The interconnection of a master MPU with various slave MPUs must be done with care to ensure valid data transfer and to avoid a situation where a slave MPU loads the data bus of the master MPU. For this reason an interface circuit is required between the master and *each* slave MPU. The PPI, in its mode 2 operation, provides the required interface. The necessary requirements of this interface circuit can be summarized as follows:

- A two-way or *bidirectional data flow* must be allowed.
- Because the transfer of data to and from the master may occur at any time, *handshaking signals* are required to ensure an orderly data flow between master and slave.
- Since the data buses of the master and slave MPU must be interfaced, tri-state buffers are required between the master MPU and the PPI (to ensure that the slave MPU does not load the master MPU data bus) and between the PPI and the slave MPU (to ensure that the data lines of the master do not load the slave MPU data bus). The first three-state buffer, on the master MPU side of the PPI, is enabled by the PPI chip select line. The second three-state buffer on the slave side of the PPI is enabled by a handshaking signal from the slave MPU when it is ready to accept data from the master.
- Data that are to be transferred from master to slave MPU must be *latched* by the interface circuit and held until the slave MPU is ready to accept the data.

7-2. PPI MODE 1 OPERATION FOR BIDIRECTIONAL DATA FLOW

Fig. 7-2 shows a schematic diagram of how the PPI can be used in its mode 1 configuration to implement the interface which is needed between a master and a slave MPU for bidirectional I/O. It must be emphasized from the outset that *the PPI is not normally configured in this way* to support bidirectional I/O between two MPUs. The reason for including the diagram is to clarify the requirements of the interface and to introduce the features of mode 2 operation.

Referring then to Fig. 7-2, the PPI has been configured with port A used for data output (and therefore to transmit data to the slave) and port B used for data input (and therefore to receive data from the slave MPU). Consider first the *transfer of data from slave to master MPU*. When the slave is ready to transmit data to the master, it must write the data into port B of the PPI which, as far as the slave is concerned, is a unique handshaking *output* port. By strobing

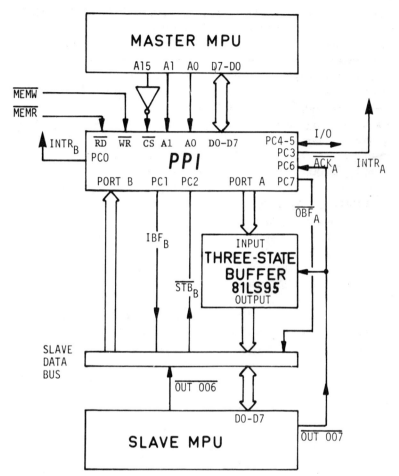

Fig. 7-2. Illustration of how the PPI could be configured in mode 1 operation to support bidirectional I/O between a master and a slave MPU.

the $\overline{\text{STB}}_B$ line with an active low device select pulse, the slave thus latches its data into port B of the PPI. The PPI responds in the usual way by raising its IBF_B line to acknowledge receipt of the data from the slave and to signal the master that a data byte is available for input. Once the master has read port B for the data byte from the slave MPU, the PPI drops its IBF_B line to signal the slave that the first data byte has been transferred and that port B can be loaded with another data byte. The data transfer just described is simply a mode 1 handshaking input operation by the master MPU using the PPI for data synchronization. The only difference between this description and that of Section 6-2, where mode 1 input was discussed, is that the source of data in this case is a second microcomputer.

Consider now the *transfer of data from master to slave*. A PPI output operation through port A in Fig. 7-2 is used. The data lines of port A cannot be connected directly to the data bus of the slave MPU, however, since port A of the PPI appears as an *input* peripheral to the slave MPU and would load its data bus. The solution, as in all microcomputer input operations, is to employ an 8-bit three-state buffer between port A and the slave MPU data bus. The mode 1 handshaking lines of port A are then used to synchronize data transfer from the master to the slave as follows. A data byte is first sent by the master to port A of the PPI in the usual way. This operation causes the $\overline{OBF}_A$ flag to go low to indicate that the data has been latched at port A. When the slave MPU detects that the $\overline{OBF}_A$ flag is low, it inputs the data that is latched at port A by enabling the three-state buffer, which is between the PPI and the slave MPU in Fig. 7-2, with a device select pulse. Note that the device select pulse is also used to strobe $\overline{ACK}_A$ and so to advise the PPI that the data at port A has been received by the slave. With $\overline{OBF}_A$ now high as a result of the $\overline{ACK}_A$ pulse, the master is free to load port A with a further byte for transfer to the slave MPU.

Hence the essential *hardware* features of this master/slave interface are:

- The need for a three-state buffer between port A and the slave MPU data bus since, as far as the slave is concerned, the data transfer just described is a simple handshaking input operation.
- The use of the port A handshaking signals to again synchronize the data flow.
- The need to connect the PPI to the master microcomputer as an I/O device. In the illustration in Fig. 7-2 the PPI was wired for memory-mapped I/O.

As a final generalization from this discussion, it should be noted that for successful master/slave data transfers both the master and the slave must monitor the IBF and $\overline{OBF}$ flags. The details of this are discussed in Section 7-4. Let us first look at how the PPI mode 2 configuration of port A achieves the same master/slave data transfers described above.

7-3. MODE 2 PPI FEATURES

In Fig. 7-3 the assignment of the lines of ports A to C is shown when port A is configured to mode 2 operation. Port A is now a bidirectional I/O port which is supported by five port C lines (PC3 to PC7) as handshaking control lines. Port B can be configured for mode 0 simple I/O (in which case the port C lines PC0–PC2 are available for input/output), or it can be configured for mode 1 handshaking input or output (in which case port C lines PC0–PC2 have their usual assignment as handshaking control lines). Let us now look more closely at port A. Fig. 7-4 shows the functional arrangement of port A when the PPI is configured for mode 2 operation. Port A is now a true bidirectional port and is designed to provide the interface between two microcomputers or between a microcomputer and a peripheral device which transmits and receives data. A floppy disc unit is an example of this type of peripheral although floppy discs are usually interfaced to a microcomputer through a dedicated floppy disc controller integrated circuit such as the Western Digital DM1771. Compare now the PPI lines in Fig. 7-2 with the mode 2 PPI lines which are illustrated in Fig. 7-4 and which are used to implement an equivalent bidirectional I/O structure. In Fig. 7-4 assume that, as in Fig. 7-2, the PPI is wired to the master MPU and that the master is therefore to the left of the PPI. In the mode 1 implementation example of Fig. 7-2 two PPI ports,

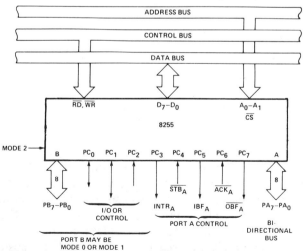

Fig. 7-3. PPI interface line assignment when port A is configured for mode 2 operation.

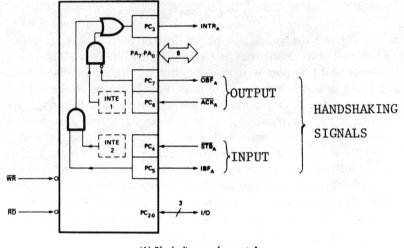

(A) Block diagram for port A.

CONTROL WORD

D_7	D_6	D_5	D_4	D_3	D_2	D_1	D_0
1	1				I/O	I/O	I/O

PC_{2-0}
1 = INPUT
0 = OUTPUT

PORT B
1 = INPUT
0 = OUTPUT

GROUP B MODE
0 = MODE 0
1 = MODE 1

(B) Mode control word.

Fig. 7-4. Functional block diagram for port A when the PPI is configured by mode control word for mode 2 operation.

A and B, were needed to effect a transfer of data in either direction between master MPU and slave MPU. In mode 2 PPI operation (Fig. 7-4), port A is configured as a true bidirectional port for data transfer between master and slave, and so frees port B for additional mode 0 or mode 1 input/output tasks associated with the master MPU. In addition, it can be seen that in both figures, the *same* sets of handshaking signals are used to synchronize data transfers. The mode 2 PPI configuration then is simply a concentration of the mode

1 implemented, bidirectional I/O interface shown in Fig. 7-2 into a single port (A) for data transfer and five lines of port C (PC7–PC3) for handshaking.

Consider now the function of each of the mode 2 handshaking control signals. For *mode 2 data input to the PPI* (this is equivalent to data transfer from slave to master MPU in Fig. 7-2):

- $\overline{STB}_A$, the *strobe* input line, loads data from the slave MPU into the port A input latch when set to a logic low.
- IBF_A, the *input buffer full* flag, is an active-high acknowledgement signal indicating that data has been loaded into the PPI's input latch.

Mode 2 data input to the PPI through port A is identical to a mode 1 input operation. The mode 2 handshaking signals, $\overline{STB}_A$ and IBF_A, are identical in meaning and function to the mode 1 input handshaking signals which were discussed in Chapter 6 and used in Fig. 7-2. The major difference between mode 2 and mode 1 input operations is in the type of device which would be wired to the lines of port A of the PPI. For mode 2 a device capable of both providing data and receiving data is connected to port A. For mode 1 a peripheral which only provides data, such as an A/D converter, would be connected to port A.

For *mode 2 data output from the PPI* (this is equivalent to data transfer from master to slave in Fig. 7-2):

- $\overline{OBF}_A$, the *output buffer full* flag, goes to a logic 0 when the master MPU has written data into the port A output latch.
- $\overline{ACK}_A$, the *acknowledge* input is sent to a logic low by the slave MPU to flag the PPI that the data latched at port A is being read. This enables the three-state output buffer of port A. Under normal conditions, $\overline{ACK}_A$ is usually at a logic high and the port A output buffer is held in its high-impedance state.

The important difference between the mode 2 and mode 1 output configurations of port A is the built-in three-state output buffer which is enabled by a logic low on the $\overline{ACK}_A$ line in mode 2 operation. This is necessary because the data held in the output latch of the PPI is an *input* to the slave MPU and must be buffered to avoid any loading of the slave MPU's data bus. Thus the effects of using the PPI in mode 2 operation as an interface between master and slave MPU's are to free port B and control lines PC0 to PC2 for other tasks and to alleviate the need for an external three-state buffer. Port

A, in mode 2 operation, functions as a data buffer between master and slave microcomputers.

The remaining functions in Fig. 7-4, namely, INTE 1, INTE 2, and $INTR_A$, are concerned with the means by which the PPI advises the master MPU that a master-to-slave transmission has been completed or that it has received data from the slave. In the first instance, $\overline{OBF}_A$ goes high to indicate that a master-to-slave data transmission has been completed. In the second instance, IBF_A goes high to indicate that the PPI has received data from the slave. In either event, $INTR_A$, the *interrupt request* flag (PC3 in Fig. 7-4) goes to logic 1 provided that INTE 1 (in the case of $\overline{OBF}_A$) or INTE 2 (in the case of IBF_A) is also high. The INTE 1 and INTE 2, *interrupt enable* flags, are internal flip-flops whose function in controlling the generation of interrupts by $\overline{OBF}_A$ and IBF_A, respectively, is similar to the function and operation of the mode 1 interrupt enable flags, $INTE_A$ and $INTE_B$. The INTE 1 and INTE 2 flags are controlled by the master MPU through bit-set/reset operations on the PPI's PC6 and PC4 bits, respectively. Hence the $INTR_A$ line can be used to interrupt the master MPU for the control of both input or output operations and, as discussed in Chapter 6, either vectored or polled interrupts can be used. For vectored interrupts, $\overline{OBF}_A$ and IBF_A can be wired

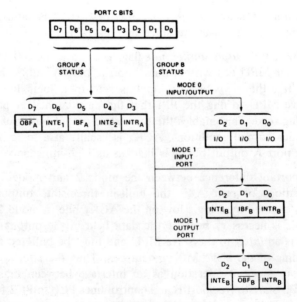

Fig. 7-5. Mode 2 status word.

to an interrupt instruction register to generate unique vector restart instructions to the master for input and output operations. When polled interrupts are used by the master MPU it must determine whether an input or output operation is to be serviced by checking the status of the IBF_A and $\overline{OBF}_A$ flags, respectively. This is done by reading port C, which provides the mode 2 status word shown in Fig. 7-5. Bits D7–D3 provide the status of bidirectional port A. Note that the assignment of D6 and D4 to INTE 1 and INTE 2 is consistent with the bit-set/reset operations on PC6 and PC4, which are required to set or reset the internal INTE 1 or INTE 2 flags, respectively.

7-4. MODE 2 PPI OPERATION AND REQUIREMENTS

(A) Hardware Requirements

Fig. 7-6 shows a typical interconnection of two microcomputers using the PPI as the interface element. The PPI is wired to the master

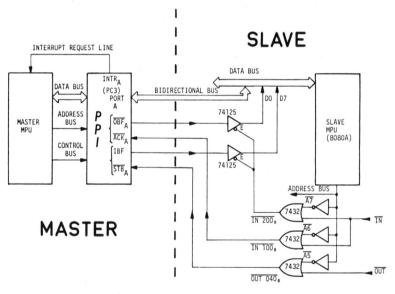

Fig. 7-6. A typical interface between master and slave microcomputers.

MPU in the usual way for either accumulator or memory-mapped I/O, and it has been configured for polled-interrupt operation by connecting its $INTR_A$ line to the interrupt input of the master MPU. The slave microcomputer is an 8080A-based system and is wired for polled operation. The major *hardware requirement* of an interface between two microcomputers is to ensure that both microcomputers are able to monitor the mode 2 handshaking flag outputs $\overline{OBF}_A$ and IBF_A of the PPI.

In this example the master MPU monitors these flags, upon receipt of an interrupt, by polling port C of the PPI for its mode 2 status word. The slave MPU is able to monitor these flags through the connection of the $\overline{OBF}_A$ and IBF_A outputs of the PPI to the slave MPU data bus through a 74125 three-state buffer integrated circuit. Note again that no external three-state buffer is needed to interface port A to the slave MPU data bus as the three-state buffer is provided internally at port A when the PPI is configured for mode 2 operation.

A *second hardware requirement* of the master-slave microcomputer interface is for the *slave* microcomputer to provide a strobe ($\overline{STB}_A$) pulse for slave-to-master data transfers and an acknowledge ($\overline{ACK}_A$) pulse for master-to-slave data transfers. In Fig. 7-6 these pulses are generated by the slave microcomputer as device select pulses $\overline{OUT}$ $\overline{040}$ and $\overline{IN\ 100}$, respectively. Note that an *output* device select pulse is required to drive the $\overline{STB}_A$ line since data are being loaded *into* port A of the PPI and therefore are output from the slave MPU. Similarly, an *input* device select pulse is required to drive the $\overline{ACK}_A$ line since data are being sent from the PPI and must therefore be input to the slave MPU.

(B) An Operational Sequence

The exact sequence of events which occurs in data transfers between master and slave, when the PPI is used as the interface element, depends of course on the tasks which are being supervised by the slave MPU. In all cases, however, the data transfers are governed by the following simple rules:

(i) In master-to-slave data transfers the behavior of the handshaking signals $\overline{OBF}$ and $\overline{ACK}$ is identical with that for mode 1 strobed output operation of the PPI.

(ii) In slave-to-master MPU data transfers the behavior of the handshaking signals $\overline{STB}$ and IBF is identical with that for mode 1 strobed input operation of the PPI.

(iii) The port A interrupt request line of the PPI, $INTR_A$, will be set by either $\overline{OBF}$ or IBF going to logic 1, provided that their respective internal interrupt enable flip-flops INTE 1 and INTE 2 are at logic 1.

Table 7-1. Sequence of Events Illustrated in the Mode 2 Timing Diagram of Fig. 7-7

Data Transfer	Action	Results
1. Master to PPI	The master MPU writes data to port A	• Leading edge of $\overline{WR}$ resets INTR flag • Trailing edge of $\overline{WR}$ sets $\overline{OBF}$ to logic low
2. Slave to PPI	The slave MPU writes data to port A by strobing $\overline{STB}$ with an output device select pulse	• Leading edge of $\overline{STB}$ sets IBF • Trailing edge of $\overline{STB}$ sets INTR flag
3. PPI to slave	The slave MPU detects $\overline{OBF}$ low and reads port A for the data from the master MPU which is held in the port A output buffer. The slave microcomputer input device select pulse is used to strobe $\overline{ACK}$	• The leading edge of $\overline{ACK}$ resets OBF high • The trailing edge of $\overline{ACK}$ sets INTR high. In this example, however, INTR is already high through Step 2 above
4. PPI to master	Responding to the interrupt from Step 2 above, the master MPU detects IBF high and reads port A for data, from the slave MPU, which is held in the port A input buffer.	• The leading edge of $\overline{RD}$ would reset INTR if $\overline{OBF}$ wasn't high • The trailing edge of $\overline{RD}$ resets IBF low

(iv) Since port A, in mode 2 operation, has an *input buffer/latch* to accept data from a slave MPU and an *output buffer/latch* to accept data from the master MPU, master-to-slave and slave-to-master data transfers may be initiated simultaneously or nearly simultaneously by the master MPU and the slave MPU, respectively.

The rules are illustrated diagrammatically in the mode 2 timing diagram which is shown in Fig. 7-7. As an example of a possible master-slave operating sequence, let us look more closely at the sequence illustrated in Fig. 7-7.

Here a master-to-slave and slave-to-master data transfer are represented. The sequence of events which is depicted in Fig. 7-7 is described in Table 7-1. You should read Table 7-1 as you examine the timing diagram in Fig. 7-7. The interesting feature of this sequence is that before the slave MPU has received the data that was transmitted to it via the PPI, the slave MPU itself initiates a transmission

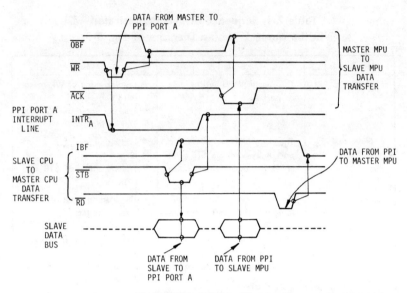

Fig. 7-7. Mode 2 timing diagram.

of data to the master MPU. Note also the way in which the PPI acts as a buffer between master and slave MPUs, and the way the handshaking signals act to resynchronize the data transfers that represent asynchronous inputs to both MPUs.

(C) Software Considerations

Our discussions so far have centered on the hardware requirements of a mode 2 PPI bidirectional interface between master and slave microcomputers. This section would be lacking, however, if mention was not made of the software required to support the interface. A discussion of the software is complicated by the need for two co-ordinated, interactive programs for the master and slave, respectively. The major concern of both sets of software is the monitoring of the PPI handshaking flags $\overline{OBF}$ and IBF. The master-slave interface of Fig. 7-6 reflects a typical allocation of the overall software of a distributed microcomputer control system. Because the master MPU will, in general, have responsibility for overall system monitoring and control, it is generally necessary for the master to service the slave only as required. For this reason an interrupt system will usually be adopted for the master MPU-to-PPI port A interface. The selection of polled or vectored interrupts is a variable which is determined by considering the trade-off between hardware requirements and response speed. Since the slave microcomputer will be dedicated to a particular task, the improved response speed (master-to-slave data transfer) of an interrupt system is usually not justified for the slave microcomputer and polling of the PPI flags by the slave MPU, as

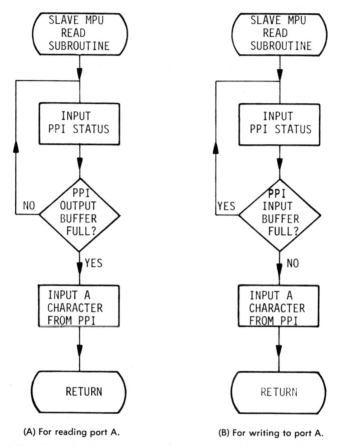

(A) For reading port A.   (B) For writing to port A.

Fig. 7-8. Flow diagrams of polling subroutines which could be used by the slave MPU in Fig. 7-6 for reading port A of the PPI and writing data to port A of the PPI.

illustrated in Fig. 7-6, is used. Because the software for the slave microcomputer is the most straightforward, let us consider this first.

Fig. 7-8 shows flowcharts of the subroutines which the slave microcomputer could used to read data from the PPI (a master-to-slave data transfer) and to write data to the PPI (a slave-to-master data transfer). The corresponding coded subroutines, which were written to fit the slave hardware configuration of Fig. 7-6, are shown in Fig. 7-9.

No new concepts are presented in the polling software that is used by the slave MPU. The mode 2 handshaking flags $\overline{\text{OBF}}$ and IBF are connected to the microcomputer data bus lines D0 and D7 (via a three-state buffer) so that their status can be easily tested by a left

```
/
/                 SLAVE SOFTWARE
/
/(A) SLAVE READ SUBROUTINE: MASTER TO SLAVE DATA TRANSFER
/
SLAVRD,  IN       / INPUT PPI FLAGS FROM
         200      /74125 TRI-STATE BUFFERS
         RAR      /SHIFT PPI OBFA FLAG(DO) INTO CARRY FLAG
         JNZ      /OBFA = "0"? IE. DATA READY FOR
                  /MASTER TO SLAVE TRANSFER
         SLAVRD   /NO? ,  TRY AGAIN
         0
         IN       /YES! INPUT A CARACTER BY STROBING
         100      /ACKA TO LOGIC LOW
         RET
```


```
/
/ (B) SLAVE WRITE SUBROUTINE : SLAVE TO MASTER DATA TRANSFER
/
SLAVWF,  IN       /INPUT PPI FLAGS FROM
         200      /74125 TRI STATE BUFFERS
         RAL      /SHIFT PPI IBFA FLAG(D7) INTO CARRY FLAG
         JZ       /IBFA = "0"? IE. IS PPI READY FOR
                  /SLAVE TO MASTER TRANSFER
         SLAVWR   /NO KEEP TRYING
         0
         OUT      /YES O/P BYTE TO PPI BY STROBING
         040      /STBA WITH AN O/P DEVICE SELECT PULSE
         RET
```

Fig. 7-9. Slave MPU software for bidirectional I/O between a master and a slave MPU using a PPI in mode 2 configuration for interfacing.

shift (for D7, the IBF flag) or a right shift (for D0, the $\overline{\text{OBF}}$ flag) of the accumulator contents into the carry flag.

The software for the master microcomputer is more difficult to generalize because of the many and varied tasks which may be required of this microcomputer in its role as the overall system supervisor and controller. The simplest situation is one in which port A of the PPI, when configured for mode 2 operation, provides the only source of system interrupts. By reading port C for the mode 2 status word and then by masking and testing bits D7 ($\overline{\text{OBF}}_A$) and D5 ($\overline{\text{IBF}}_A$) in turn, the master MPU can determine whether the PPI has received data from the slave microcomputer ($\overline{\text{IBF}}_A$ high) or whether the slave MPU has successfully read data which the master had sent to port A ($\overline{\text{OBF}}$ high). In the first case, where the "input buffer full" flag of the PPI is high, the master MPU reads port A for data which was sent from the slave and which is held at port A. The master then processes this data and returns to its main task.

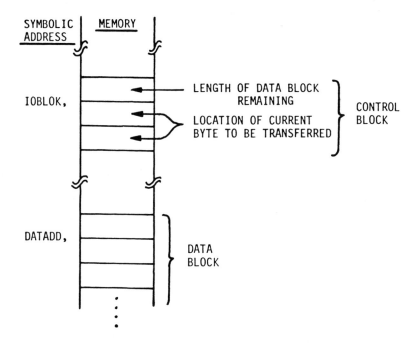

Fig. 7-10. Schematic illustration of a simple interrupt control block for a write operation by the master to the PPI.

In the second case the $\overline{\text{OBF}}_A$ flag generates an interrupt by returning to a logic high. This implies that the data, which was sent to the PPI by the master, has been successfully read by the slave MPU and that the output buffer of port A is empty. The response of the master MPU depends upon whether a single byte or a block of data was to be sent to the slave MPU. One approach to handling these two possibilities is to set up a *control block* in memory. This is illustrated in Fig. 7-10 and, in the simplest case, would consist of the number of data bytes remaining to be transferred to the slave MPU, and of the address in memory of the location of the *current* byte which is to be transferred. Initially, the main task software must load the control block with the *length* of the data block which is to be transferred to the slave and the *starting location* in memory of the data block, and to enable the INTE 1, interrupt enable flip-flop. This is illustrated in Fig. 7-11 which gives flowcharts for the main task and for the interrupt service subroutine. With INTE 1 enabled (*cf* Fig. 7-4) and the PPI output buffer empty ($\overline{OBF}$ high), an interrupt will be generated by the PPI. The interrupt software polls the status of the PPI and, when the output buffer of port A is found to be empty, a data byte for the slave is written to the PPI. The address in memory of this byte is found in the control block. The counter representing the length of the data block is decremented and stored at the beginning of the control block. The new value of the counter, representing the number of bytes remaining to be transferred, is checked and, if nonzero, the INTE 1 flag is re-enabled (both INTE 1 and INTE 2 are disabled at the beginning of the subroutine). If the counter is zero, the INTE 1 flag is left disabled, thus preventing further interrupts from $\overline{OBF}_A$. When a further data block is to be sent to the slave CPU, the main task software would again initialize the control block with the block length and the starting address of the new data, and enable INTE 1. The data would then be transferred under interrupt control as described above and as illustrated in the flowchart which is shown in Fig. 7-11. The software corresponding to these flowcharts is given in Fig. 7-12.

In microcomputer systems which supervise a number of input and output tasks under interrupt control, an expanded control block may be required for each peripheral. Additional control information may include:

- The *type* of I/O, viz, input or output.
- The status of the current I/O transaction, i.e., busy or complete.
- The address of a subroutine which will be called after the I/O block has been performed.
- Other parameters associated with the particular input or output task.

Further details on typical applications of this software technique for managing interrupts are given in Intel Corporation's Application Notes for their SBC 80/10 microcomputer and their 8255 PPI (see Section 7-6).

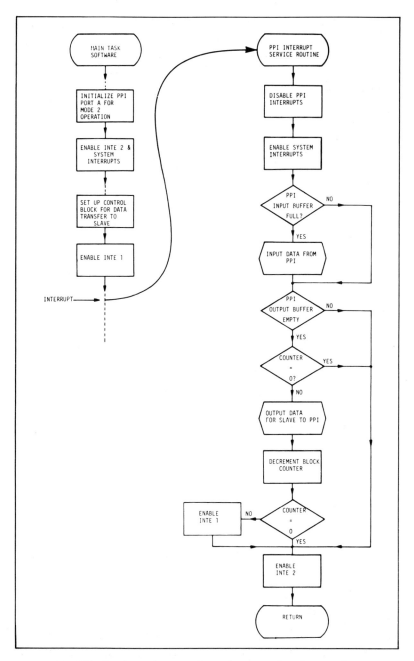

Fig. 7-11. Flowcharts of master software for master-slave data transfers.

MASTER SOFTWARE

(A) MAIN TASK SOFTWARE ASSOCIATED WITH MASTER/SLAVE
    DATA TRANSFERS

```
MAIN,   NOP
          .
          .
          .
          .
        MVIA      /LOAD ACCUMULATOR WITH PPI MODE CONTROL
        OUT       /OUTPUT MODE CONTROL WORD TO PPI
        CNTRL     /CONTROL REGISTER
        MVIA      /LOAD ACCUMULATOR WITH BIT SET CONTROL WORD
        PC4SET    /FOR PC4-INTE 2
        OUT       /OUTPUT IT TO THE CONTROL REGISTER
        CNTRL
        EI        /ENABLE SYSTEM INTERUPTS
          .
          .
          .
          .
          .
          .
          .
        LXIH      /LOAD H,L REGISTERS WITH ADDRESS POINTER
        IOBLOK    /TO THE BEGINNING OF THE MASTER TO
        0         /SLAVE WRITE CONTROL BLOCK
        MVIM      /WRITE THE DATA BLOCK BYTE NUMBER
        001       /TO THE FIRST LOCATION IN THE WRITE
        LXIH      /CONTROL BLOCK.LOAD H,L WITH ADDRESS
        DATADD    /OF BEGINNING OF DATA BLOCK
        0
        SHLD      /STORE THIS ADDRESS IN
        IOBLOK+1  /THE WRITE CONTROL BLOCK
        0         /
        MVIA      /LOAD ACCUMULATOR WITH THE BIT SET CONTROL
        PC6SET    /WORD FOR PC6-INTE 1
        OUT       /OUTPUT IT TO THE CONTROL REGISTER
        CNTRL
          .
          .
          .
          .
          .
PPIINT,  PUSHPSW  /SAVE MICROCOMPUTER STATUS
         PUSHH
         PUSHB
         MVIA     /DISABLE PPI INTERRUPTS
         PC6RST
         OUT
         CNTRL
         MVIA
         PC4RST
         OUT
         CNTRL
```

Fig. 7-12. Main task software associated

```
          EI        /ENABLE SYSTEM INTERRUPTS
          IN        /INPUT PPI STATUS WORD
          PORTC
          MOVBA     /SAVE STATUS WORD
          ANI       /MASK IBFA:- BIT D5
          040
          JZ        /IS INPUT BUFFER FULL (IBF='1')
          POINTA    /NO, TRY STATUS OF OUTPUT BUFFER
          0
          IN        /YES, INPUT BYTE FROM PORT A
          PORTA
          CALL      /AND PROCESS IT
          PROCESS
          0
POINTA,   MOVAB     /RESTORE PPI STATUS WORD
          ANI       /MASK OBFA-BIT D7
          200
          JZ        /IS OUTPUT BUFFER EMPTY (OBF='1')
          POINTB    /NO, RETURN
          0
          LDA       /CHECK IF COUNTER IS ZERO
          IOBLOK    /SO THAT OUTPUT CODE CAN
          0         /BE BYPASSED IF INTERRUPT
          ORI       /WAS FOR AN INPUT
          000
          JZ
          POINTB
          0
          LHLD      /LOAD CURRENT ADDRESS OF DATA BYTE
          IOBLOK+1
          0
          MOVAM     /INPUT THE DATA BYTE FROM MEMORY TO A
          OUT       /OUTPUT DATA BYTE TO PORT A
          PORTA
          INXH      /POINT TO ADRESS OF NEXT BYTE
          SHLD      /STORE ADDRESS OF NEXT BYTE IN THE
          IOBLOK+1/CONTROL BLOCK
          LXIH      /POINT TO BYTE COUNTER
          IOBLOK
          0
          MOVAM     /INPUT BYTE COUNTER
          DCRA      /DECREMENT COUNTER
          MOVMA     /WRITE RESULT TO MEMORY
          JZ        /COUNTER ZERO?
          POINTB    /YES, RETURN
          0
          MVIA      /NO, LOAD ACCUMULATOR WITH CONTROL BYTE TO
          PC6SET    /SET PC6=INTE 1
          OUT       /OUTPUT TO CONTROL REGISTER
          CNTRL
POINTB,   MVIA      /ENABLE INTE 2=PC4
          PC4SET
          OUT
          CNTRL
          POPB      /RESTOR STATUS OF MICROCOMPUTER
          POPH
          POPPSW
          RET
```

with master-slave data transfers.

7-5. AN APPLICATION

In the previous section the hardware and software required to interface two microcomputers were detailed using the mode 2 operation of the PPI as the interface. The purpose of this section is to illustrate a typical environment in which distributed microcomputer control is useful, and to illustrate the type of data which would need to be transferred between MPUs on the bidirectional bus. The example is taken from the area of digital microcomputer control of an industrial process. The schematic diagram of Fig. 7-13 shows part of the overall process. A larger microcomputer system is used as the overall process supervisor while small dedicated microcomputers are distributed throughout the plant to provide localized control of small portions of the overall process. The main supervising microcomputer would probably be located in the process control room. In addition to a large read/write memory and floppy disc capability for program and data storage, this master microcomputer would typically control several video display units (VDUs) or cathode ray terminals (crt's), both within the control room and at stations throughout the plant, as well as the process control panel and board. The VDUs would be used for system interrogation to determine the system status in terms of plots, histograms, tabulations, etc.

In the illustration of Fig. 7-13, the microcomputer is being used for pressure and temperature control. Typical data, which would be sent to the slave microcomputer by the master, would include upper and lower limits, as well as set point values, for the bath temperature and the pressures in the two gas lines shown. The slave would then be responsible for controlling the temperature within the limits sent by the master as well as for switching from one gas line to another when, say, the line 1 pressure dropped below the lower limit set by the master. In cases where the pressure and temperature limits exceed those sent by the master, the slave could send an alarm or flag back to the master. A task completed flag could be sent when the temperature and pressures stabilized. Additional tasks for the slave would include the periodic logging and display of the local pressures and temperatures. This data would be passed back to the master at periods depending upon the storage capacity (usually minimal) of the slave microcomputer. Throughout the process cycle the master microcomputer would monitor the temperature and pressure data from the slave as well as the alarm and task completed flags and send updated limits and setpoints to the slave as the process variables

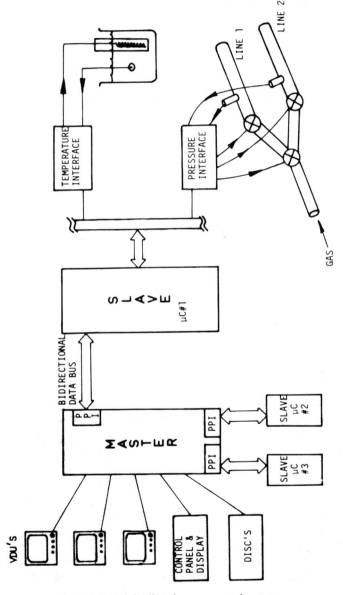

Fig. 7-13. Typical distributed process control system.

in other parts of the process changed. The alarm flag from the slave would necessarily be monitored closely by the master so that in the event of problems arising, the master could take action to alter process parameters elsewhere in the plant.

7-6. REFERENCES

Ebright, A., "8255 Programmable Peripheral Interface Applications," *Intel Application Note AP-15*.

Rolander, T., "SBC 80/10—System 80/10 Single Board Computer Applications," *Intel Application Note AP-26* (1977).

7-7. SUMMARY OF EXPERIMENT 7-1

Experiment	*Description*
7-1	In this experiment two 8080 microcomputers are interfaced for bidirectional I/O using the PPI in its mode 2 operation. The sequential transfer of data from master MPU to slave MPU and back again to the master is illustrated.

EXPERIMENT 7-1
A BIDIRECTIONAL INTERFACE BETWEEN A MASTER AND A SLAVE MICROCOMPUTER: POLLED OPERATION

Purpose

The aims of this experiment are as follows:

a. To interface two 8080-based microcomputers for bidirectional I/O using a PPI which is configured for mode 2 polled operation.

b. To illustrate a sequential transfer of data from master MPU to slave MPU and back again to the master.

Discussion

In this experiment the master and slave microcomputers will be interfaced using the technique which was described in the text for this chapter. Both the master and slave microcomputers monitor the bidirectional I/O handshaking signals IBF and $\overline{OBF}$ by *polling* their status. Note, however, from the circuit for the interface that the slave microcomputer inputs IBF and $\overline{OBF}$ on data lines D1 and D0 respectively in this experiment.

Pin Configurations of the Integrated Circuits (Fig. 7-14)

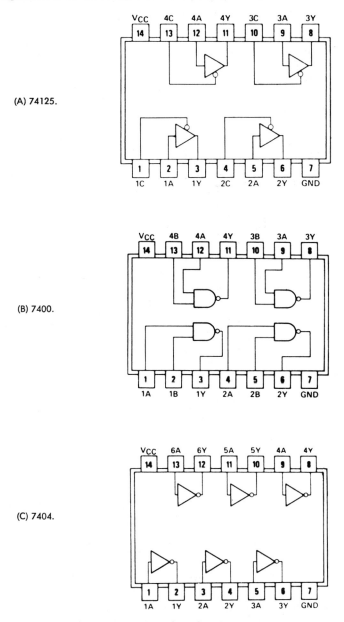

(A) 74125.

(B) 7400.

(C) 7404.

Fig. 7-14. IC pin configurations.

Schematic Diagram of the Circuit (Fig. 7-15)

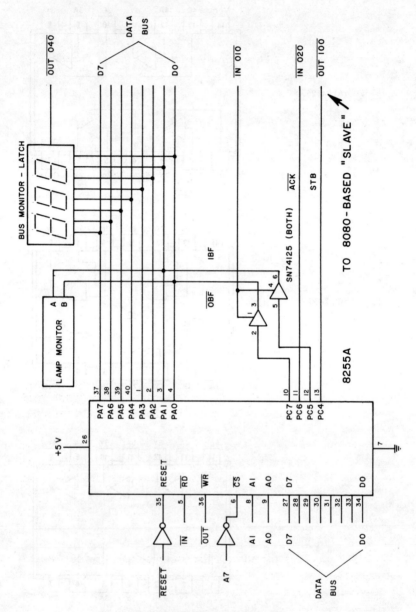

Fig. 7-15. Circuit for Experiment 7-1.

Fig. 7-16 shows, in block diagram form, the path of the sequential flow of data between master and slave which will be implemented. Data will be transferred from the master MPU to the PPI, thence to the slave microcomputer which will increment the data byte and transmit it back to the master via the PPI. The master then increments the received byte and retransmits it to the slave. The objective is to program both master and slave microcomputers so that this data exchange can be easily monitored.

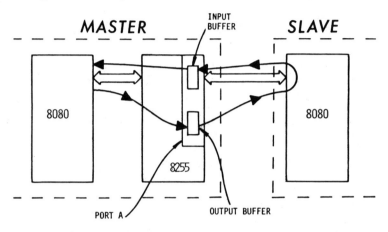

Fig. 7-16. Block diagram of the interconnection of master and slave MPUs showing the data path for Objective b of the experiment.

To do this it is necessary to introduce delays in both the master and slave software to ensure that several seconds elapse between reception and retransmission of data by both the master and the slave. The timing diagram for the data exchange (Fig. 7-17) shows four stable states and the tasks of both the master and slave software have been noted for each of the states. The software in Figs. 7-18 and 7-19 for the master and the slave microcomputers implements these tasks.

Procedure

Step 1

The first step is to connect the interface between the two microcomputers that are to be used as the master and the slave. This can be done in two steps. First, interface a PPI to the microcomputer, designated as the master, for accumulator input/output. Most probably this task will have already been completed for experiments in

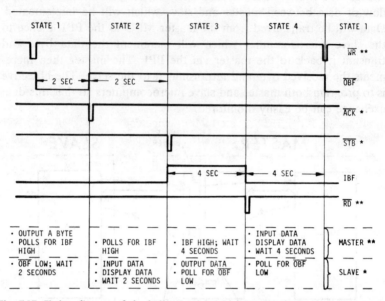

Fig. 7-17. Timing diagram of the bidirectional handshaking signals for the exchange of data between master and slave which is illustrated in Fig. 7-16.

earlier chapters. Second, wire PPI lines PA7–PA0 and PC7–PC4 to the slave microcomputer as shown in the circuit diagram (Fig. 7-15). As part of this exercise, the following device select pulses must be decoded:

$$\overline{\text{IN 010}} \qquad \overline{\text{OUT 040}}$$
$$\overline{\text{IN 020}} \qquad \overline{\text{OUT 100}}$$

Since the slave microcomputer requires no additional device select pulses, single address line or lineal decoding can be implemented with the circuits in Fig. 7-20. Use these circuits to complete the interfacing of the slave microcomputer to the PPI. Be sure that there is a good ground connection in common between both computer systems!

Step 2

Study the programs for the master and slave microcomputers in conjunction with Fig. 7-17. In particular, for both master and slave software, identify the sections of code corresponding to each of the four states which are identified in Fig. 7-17. In the master software an endless loop has been inserted in the program at location "HERE"

(020 011). This loop is used to effectively halt the program during initial testing of the interface (STEP 5). It will then be removed for proper master/slave interaction.

Step 3

In the master software, symbolic names PORTA, PORTC, and CNTRL have been used to represent the device codes for port A, port C, and the control register of the PPI, respectively. These symbolic names have been equated with device codes 204, 206, and 207, respectively. For the master microcomputer to PPI interface, determine the device codes for port A, port C, and the control register. Now replace our device codes in the master program with the appropriate ones for your PPI interface, if necessary.

Step 4

By referring to the mode control word format of Fig. 2-2A, verify that 300 is a suitable code for initializing the PPI for mode 2 operation.

Step 5

Load the master and slave microcomputers with the respective programs that are provided. Execute the program stored in the master microcomputer. What do you observe on the lamp monitors? What is the program in the master microcomputer doing? Can you see why this step has been included? Note your answers in the space below.

When the master software was run, it was observed that both the $\overline{OBF}$ and the IBF flags took up initial logic 0 states. The program has been effectively halted at location HERE due to the tight loop. This allows the bidirectional I/O handshaking flags to be monitored. It is necessary to know the initial values for $\overline{OBF}$ and IBF in this example to ensure an ordered sequential data transfer as described in Fig. 7-17. If IBF, in particular, is at logic 1 on initialization, state 2 in the diagram would be missed entirely. This would not invalidate the data transfer sequence, but it would make the flags more difficult to observe. If IBF does initialize to logic 1 in your PPI, replace the jump instruction at location HERE with

Programs

(A) Master Software (Fig. 7-18)

```
                    /
                    /MASTER SOFTWARE: POLLING.
                    /
                    DW STACK 024 000
                    DW TIMOUT 000 277
                    DB PORTA 204
                    DB PORTC 206
                    DB CNTRL 207
                    DB MODE 300
                    *020 000
020 000 061  MSTART,  LXISP
020 001 000           STACK
020 002 024           0
020 003 076           MVIA      /INITIALIZE PPI FOR MODE 2 OPERATION
020 004 300           MODE
020 005 323           OUT
020 006 207           CNTRL
020 007 006           MVIB
020 010 000           000
020 011 303  HERE,    JMP
020 012 011           HERE
020 013 020           0
020 014 170  LOOP1,   MOVAB     /RESTORE BYTE
020 015 074           INRA
020 016 323           OUT       /AND OUTPUT TO PORT A
020 017 204           PORTA
020 020 333  LOOP2,   IN        /GET PPI STATUS
020 021 206           PORTC
020 022 346           ANI       /CHECK INPUT BUFFER FLAG(PC5)
020 023 040           040
020 024 312           JZ        /IS PORT A INPUT BUFFER FULL?
020 025 020           LOOP2     /NO,TRY AGAIN
020 026 020           0
020 027 315           CALL      /YES, WAIT 4 SECONDS
020 030 045           FORSEC
020 031 020           0
020 032 333           IN        /NOW INPUT BYTE FROM SLAVE
020 033 204           PORTA
020 034 107           MOVBA     /STORE BYTE
020 035 323           OUT       /AND DISPLAY IT
020 036 000           000
020 037 315           CALL
020 040 045           FORSEC
020 041 020           0
020 042 303           JMP       /LOOP TO SEND THE BYTE TO THE SLAVE
020 043 014           LOOP1
020 044 020           0
```

Fig. 7-18. Master software

This will clear the IBF flag. Otherwise replace the code at locations 011, 012, and 013 with NOPs i.e., 000.

Step 6

Reset the master microcomputer and commence program execution. What do you observe this time?

You should observe that $\overline{OBF}$ has been reset to logic 0, indicating that the master software has loaded the PPI with a byte for the slave microcomputer. The master microcomputer is in state 1 (Fig. 7-17).

Step 7

Now execute the slave microcomputer program. What do you observe? Is this consistent with the timing diagram of Fig. 7-17? Note your observations below.

```
        /
        /DELAY SUBROUTINE "FORSEC"
        /DESCRIPTION: THIS SUBROUTINE GENERATES A FOUR(4)
        /             SECOND DELAY. ALL REGISTERS ARE
        /             SAVED.
        /
020 045 365  FORSEC, PUSHPSW /SAVE MASTER STATUS
020 046 345          PUSHH
020 047 305          PUSHB
020 050 325          PUSHD
020 051 001          LXIB    /LOAD TIMING WORD
020 052 310          310     /FOR A 4 SEC. DELAY
020 053 001          001
020 054 315  LOOPA,  CALL
020 055 277          TIMOUT
020 056 000          0
020 057 013          DCXB
020 060 170          MOVAB
020 061 261          ORAC
020 062 302          JNZ
020 063 054          LOOPA
020 064 020          0
020 065 321          POPD    /RESTORE MASTER STATUS
020 066 301          POPB
020 067 341          POPH
020 070 361          POPPSW
020 071 311          RET
```

for Experiment 7-1.

If you are using MMD-1 type microcomputer for the master and the slave, you will observe the byte at port 0 of the master being incremented by two each time IBF goes from logic 1 to logic 0. This should occur approximately once per 12 seconds. Similarly, the octal display, which is driven by the slave microcomputer, will increment with respect to the value displayed at port 0 of the master each time $\overline{OBF}$ goes from logic 0 to logic 1. Again this should be approximately once per 12 seconds.

If the displays are increasing as described above and the handshaking flags are following the pattern of Fig. 7-17, you have successfully interfaced two microcomputers!

Step 8

Note in the following space the locations in the master and the slave software at which the received byte is incremented.

In the master software the INRA instruction is at location 020 015. In the slave software the INRA instruction is at location 003 024.

Now try removing either of these instructions and executing the programs. Be sure, when starting up the programs, to execute the master software first. With one of the INRA instructions removed, the displays will increment by 1. Replace the INTA instructions with DCRA instructions. You should be able to predict the effect of this change and to confirm your prediction.

Step 9

As a final exercise, write in the following space the location in read/write memory of the call to the 4-second delay in the master

(B) Slave Software (Fig. 7-19)

```
                 /
                 /SLAVE SOFTWARE
                 /
                 DW STACK 004 000
                 DW TIMOUT 000 277
                 *003 000
003 000 061          LXISP
003 001 000          STACK
003 002 004          0
003 003 333    START,  IN      /INPUT PPI FLAGS
003 004 010          010
003 005 346          ANI     /PPI OUTPUT BUFFER FULL?
003 006 001          001
003 007 302          JNZ     /NO,TRY AGAIN
003 010 003          START
003 011 003          0
003 012 315          CALL    /YES,WAIT 2 SECS.
003 013 032          TWOSEC
003 014 003          0
003 015 333          IN      /INPUT DATA FROM PORT A
003 016 020          020
003 017 323          OUT     /DISPLAY DATA
003 020 040          040
003 021 315          CALL
003 022 032          TWOSEC
003 023 003          0
003 024 074          INRA    /INCARMENT BYTE
003 025 323          OUT     /SEND BYTE TO MASTER
003 026 100          100
003 027 303          JMP     /JUMP TO INPUT BYTE FROM MASTER
003 030 003          START
003 031 003          0
                 /
                 /
                 /
                 /
                 /DELAY SUBROUTINE "TWOSEC"
                 /DESCRIPTION: THIS SUBROUTINE GENERATES A TWO(2) SECOND
                 /            DELAY.ALL REGISTERS ARE SAVED.
                 /
                 /
003 032 365    TWOSEC,  PUSHPSW /SAVE SLAVE STATUS
003 033 345          PUSHH
003 034 305          PUSHB
003 035 325          PUSHD
003 036 016          MVIC    /LOAD TIMING BYTE
003 037 310          310     /FOR A 2 SEC. DELAY
003 040 315    LOOPA,  CALL
003 041 277          TIMOUT
003 042 000          0
003 043 015          DCRC
003 044 302          JNZ
003 045 040          LOOPA
003 046 003          0
003 047 321          POPD    /RESTORE SLAVE STATUS
003 050 301          POPB
003 051 341          POPH
003 052 361          POPPSW
003 053 311          RET
```

Fig. 7-19. Slave software for Experiment 7-1.

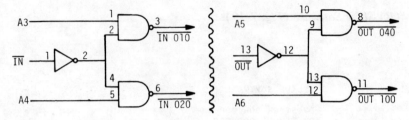

Fig. 7-20. Circuits for single address line or lineal decoding.

software which generates state 4; and write the location of the call to the 2-second delay in the slave software which generates state 2.

For state 4 the master software call is at location 020 037. For state 2 the slave software call is at location 003 021. Replace these calls with NOPs and again execute master and slave software, commencing with the master software. Have states 2 and 4 been removed? They should have.

Questions

1. Draw a timing diagram similar to Fig. 7-17 for the following four-state sequence:

   (a) Master outputs a byte to PPI.
   (b) Slave outputs a byte to PPI.
   (c) Master inputs a byte from PPI.
   (d) Slave inputs a byte from PPI.

2. Modify the master and slave software to generate this data transfer sequence.

Appendix 1

Electrical Characteristics and Timing Diagrams For the 8255*

* *Courtesy of Intel Corporation*

D.C. CHARACTERISTICS $T_A = 0°C$ to $70°C$; $V_{CC} = +5V \pm 5\%$; $V_{SS} = 0V$

Symbol	Parameter	Min.	Typ.	Max.	Unit	Test Conditions
V_{IL}	Input Low Voltage			.8	V	
V_{IH}	Input High Voltage	2.0			V	
V_{OL}	Output Low Voltage			.4	V	$I_{OL} = 1.6mA$
V_{OH}	Output High Voltage	2.4			V	$I_{OH} = -50\mu A$ ($-100\mu A$ for D.B. Port)
I_{OH}[1]	Darlington Drive Current		2.0		mA	$V_{OH} = 1.5V$, $R_{EXT} = 390\Omega$
I_{CC}	Power Supply Current		40		mA	

NOTE:
1. Available on 8 pins only.

A.C. CHARACTERISTICS $T_A = 0°C$ to $70°C$; $V_{CC} = +5V \pm 6\%$; $V_{SS} = 0V$

Symbol	Parameter	Min.	Typ.	Max.	Unit	Test Condition
t_{WP}	Pulse Width of $\overline{WR}$			430	ns	
t_{DW}	Time D.B. Stable Before $\overline{WR}$	10			ns	
t_{WD}	Time D.B. Stable After $\overline{WR}$	65			ns	
t_{AW}	Time Address Stable Before $\overline{WR}$	20			ns	
t_{WA}	Time Address Stable After $\overline{WR}$	35			ns	
t_{CW}	Time CS Stable Before $\overline{WR}$	20			ns	
t_{WC}	Time CS Stable After $\overline{WR}$	35			ns	
t_{WB}	Delay From $\overline{WR}$ To Output			500	ns	
t_{RP}	Pulse Width of $\overline{RD}$	430			ns	
t_{IR}	$\overline{RD}$ Set-Up Time	50			ns	
t_{HR}	Input Hold Time	50			ns	
t_{RD}	Delay From $\overline{RD} = 0$ To System Bus	350			ns	
t_{OD}	Delay From $\overline{RD} = 1$ To System Bus	150			ns	
t_{AR}	Time Address Stable Before $\overline{RD}$	50			ns	
t_{CR}	Time $\overline{CS}$ Stable Before $\overline{RD}$	50			ns	
t_{AK}	Width Of $\overline{ACK}$ Pulse	500			ns	
t_{ST}	Width Of $\overline{STB}$ Pulse	350			ns	
t_{PS}	Set-Up Time For Peripheral	150			ns	
t_{PH}	Hold Time For Peripheral	150			ns	
t_{RA}	Hold Time for A_1, A_0 After $\overline{RD} = 1$	379			ns	
t_{RC}	Hold Time For CS After $\overline{RD} = 1$	5			ns	
t_{AD}	Time From $\overline{ACK} = 0$ To Output (Mode 2)			500	ns	
t_{KD}	Time From $\overline{ACK} = 1$ To Output Floating			300	ns	
t_{WO}	Time From $\overline{WR} = 1$ To $\overline{OBF} = 0$			300	ns	
t_{AO}	Time From $\overline{ACK} = 0$ To $\overline{OBF} = 1$			500	ns	
t_{SI}	Time From $\overline{STB} = 0$ To IBF			600	ns	
t_{RI}	Time From $\overline{RD} = 1$ To IBF $= 0$			300	ns	

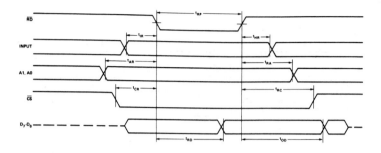

Mode 0 (Basic Input)

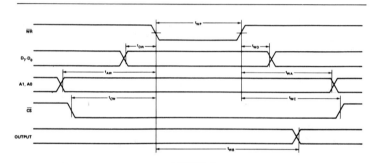

Mode 0 (Basic Output)

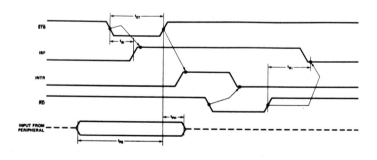

Mode 1 (Strobed Input)

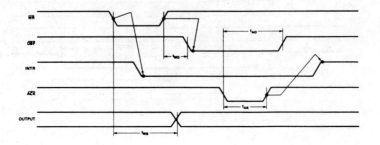

Mode 1 (Strobed Output)

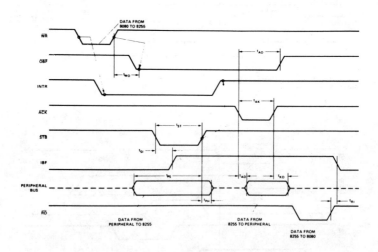

MODE 2 (BI-DIRECTIONAL INPUT/OUTPUT)

Appendix 2

8255 Control Word and Status Word Summary*

* *Courtesy of Intel Corporation*

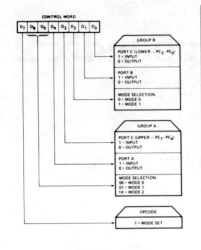

MODE CONTROL WORD

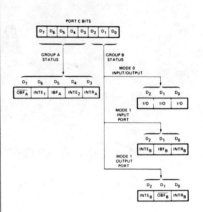

MODE 2 STATUS WORD

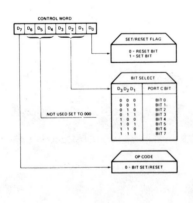

BIT SET/RESET CONTROL WORD

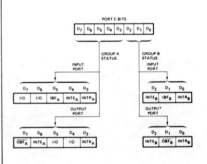

MODE 1 STATUS WORD

Index

TO THE READER

This book is one of an expanding series of books that will cover the field of basic electronics and digital electronics from basic gates and flip-flops through microcomputers and digital telecommunications. We are attempting to develop a mailing list of individuals who would like to receive information on the series. We would be delighted to add your name to it if you would fill in the information below and mail this sheet to us. Thanks.

1. I have the following books:

_____

_____

_____

_____

_____

_____

_____

_____

_____

_____

_____

2. My occupation is: ☐ student   ☐ teacher, instructor   ☐ hobbyist

☐ housewife   ☐ scientist, engineer, doctor, etc.   ☐ businessman

☐ Other: _____

Name (print): _____

Address _____

City _____   State _____

Zip Code _____

Mail to:

Books
P.O. Box 715
Blacksburg, Virginia 24060